UNWRAPPING THE GIFTS OF GRACE

I read this book with much interest and had been waiting for such a book on Charismatic Movement theology as someone who had lived in it at its early stage and who remains attached to it to this day. The book gives a fundamental theological foundation to Charismatic Movement, particularly of the African Churches. Moreover, it serves to correct and guide Evangelical Churches to recognize the Charismatic gifts within their ministries for edification and all-around growth.

Reverend Iteffa Gobena Molte

President Emeritus, Ethiopian Evangelical Church, Mekane Yesus (EECMY)

President (2000-2008)

Rev. Fogi's book on the gifts of grace is itself a gift from above in a broader sense. He clearly narrated his own journey with the living Spirit of Jesus and how God's Spirit has manifested the gifts in his life and the people around him. His biblical claims on the subject, coupled with firm doctrinal positions and contextual insights, make the writing compelling. Furthermore, Rev. Fogi's work adds one of the most useful resources that leverages global south Christianity's stories and passion to strengthen the partnership with the larger body of Christ. Though disagreements are inevitable on such a deeper theological and experiential conversations, the book is indeed inspiring and directional to exhibit a fulfilling life as disciples of Jesus.

Yared Halche, PhD

Executive Director, Mobilizing Witness

Southeastern District, LCMS

"Misio Dei, Soli Deo Gloria!"

I have had the distinct privilege of knowing the Reverend Teka Fogi for over twenty years, both as a colleague and a dear friend. Being deeply rooted in an unwavering Christology, while simultaneously being a passionate proclaimer of the Gospel, Teka is uniquely qualified (and I believe called) to present this thorough yet concise publication regarding the work of the Third Person of the Trinity.

Unwrapping the Gifts of Grace is a clear distillation of the history, theology, and biblical grounding for "unwrapping" and then practicing the Gifts of the Holy Spirit within the context of worship... and beyond! Not only that, but also it's a heartfelt reflection of his own personal journey in Christ and witnessing supernatural encounters of the inbreaking of the Kingdom of God. Part of what makes this book timely—and so fiercely needed—is knowing that our present-day culture is becoming more and more of a neo-pagan society, while at the same time the Church across denominational lines is faltering and has grown complacent. The only hope for such a time and place is for the Church to operate in the fullness and power of the Holy Spirit.

Teka's book is a field manual for the local church to equip its pastors and leaders faithfully and effectively to first engage and then mobilize their respective church members (or missional disciples) with the full armor of God (cf. Ephesians 6:10-17) and into the complete implementation of the Gifts of the Spirit (cf. 1 Corinthians 12). Perhaps then the Church will begin to witness a greater harvest, as the laborers are dispatched into a world in desperate need of a Savior (cf. Matthew 9:35-38)!

I encourage readers as they accept the challenge presented within these pages to reconsider our dire need for the wondrous work of the Spirit, for such an hour as this. May the Lord grant you the wisdom to step boldly into Pastor Teka's gracious invitation.

Reverend K. Craig Moorman
Pastor/Mission Developer, River's Edge Ministries NALC/LCMC
Author, *The Awe-full Privilege: This Thing Called Parenting*
Board Member, Lutheran CORE

This book is a treasure! Teka's personal story and journey are inspiring, his research and historical overview of the Charismatic Movement through the lens of Lutheran understanding is thoughtful and thorough, and his handling of the work of the Holy Spirit and the spiritual gifts that God gives are faithful scripturally and solid theologically. Having had the privilege of working extensively in Ethiopia for the past fifteen years, I believe Teka's book is going to be a tremendous resource and helpful tool for Christians all over the world who wish to faithfully understand, receive, and use all the gifts that God gives to His Church for the purpose of fulfilling His Mission.

Dr. Scott F. Rische
PLI International

The very title of this book sets the course for the correct interpretation of the Biblical teaching on the gifts listed by St. Paul in 1 Corinthians 12 and other New Testament passages. Clarifying the work of the Holy Spirit and his gifting of Christians with various gifts is an act of grace. Therefore, any of the gifts mentioned in the New Testament are to be received as gifts of unmerited grace. And as such, they are to use, not for oneself, but for others—especially those in the house of faith. This book can be helpful not just in Ethiopia, but also around the world and especially where the Gospel is breaking through pagan and darkened cultures.

Norbert Oesch
PLI International

UNWRAPPING THE GIFTS OF GRACE

A Biblical and Theological Perspective

TEKA OBSA FOGI

TENTH POWER

ELGIN, IL • TYLER, TX

TENTHPOWERPUBLISHING
www.tenthpowerpublishing.com

Cover design: Amanuel Wolteji
Interior Design: Larry Taylor

Softcover ISBN 978-1-938840-60-9

e-book ISBN 978-1-938840-61-6

10 9 8 7 6 5 4 3 2 1

CONTENTS

ACKNOWLEDGMENTS

Above all, I am grateful to the almighty God for helping me to write this book. This was really what I wanted to do all along. Next, I want to acknowledge the pain my wife took that ministry presented in our almost 35 years together a ministers of the gospel. The absence from home to minister to the church, the economic pressure we experienced throughout my tenure as a pastor, and the conflicts we suffered brought a lot of pain. I want to appreciate Tenagne Negussie Woldeyohannes for enduring all with me throughout the years. I must appreciate my daughter Efrata Teka Obsa for her encouragement and financial support for this project. The book could have not been published if she didn't make a *significant* financial contribution. Apart from that, the ORELC members' response to my request for financial support is what gave me the confidence to finally push through the publication of this book.

The Oromo Resurrection Evangelical Lutheran Church (ORELC) is where I grew up as a Christian and a pastor. God taught me many things in the fellowship of this church, through weaknesses and times of success. Volunteer ministers and members of the church have nurtured me with their love and encouragement throughout the time I was their pastor.

The palpable love I experienced among ORELC members surpasses the pain I suffered in ministering in this church. God has filled my mind with blessings and the desire to study the Scriptures. He enlightened me as I dedicated my time on the pages of the Scriptures. The members of ORELC and non-members who attended service at ORELC have fed me with their love. They bore with me my weaknesses and encouraged me to serve the Lord among them. I learned a lot by trying to teach them.

I just want to say, "Thank you, ORELC!"

My friend Dr. Tesfai Tesema led me to Dr. Jim Galvin, who is in charge of the publishing agency Tenth Power Publishing. Dr. Galvin did a wonderful job giving the book a beautiful and easy-to-read look. Dr. Yared Halche introduced me to Dr. Robert Scudiery, who in turn introduced me to Mrs. Christy Piney, a very effective editor who edited this book for a very reasonable pay. I also want to say thank you to Craig Moorman, a fellow pastor, for his persistent friendship since I arrived in the United States.

I want to dedicate this book to all members of the Oromo
Resurrection Evangelical Lutheran Church (ORELC),
including the infants I baptized in the church.
May God Bless you all.

INTRODUCTION

I was born to a peasant father and a homemaking mother in Illubabor Zone in the present-day Oromia Regional State in southwest Ethiopia. My parents were followers of Waaqeffannaa, the Oromo Traditional Religion (OTR). They were also baptized in the Ethiopian Orthodox Church but had little knowledge about that faith.

The OTR believes in one all-powerful, ever-present, omnipresent, and all-knowing creator, Waaqayyoo. Waaqayyoo is a strictly monotheistic Unitarian god. The OTR also allows ancestral spirits like Ayyaana Haadhaa (the spirit or grace of one's own mother) and Ayyaana Abbaa (the spirit or grace of one's own father) to be mediators between the worshiper and Waaqayyoo after the death of the worshiper's parents. The version of the Oromo Traditional Religion followed by my clan, the Buyaa Jaanjaroo, makes sacrifices to demons, especially those that live in the mountains, big rivers, and trees.

I came from this background to faith in Jesus Christ our Lord through two very important personal experiences that totally transformed the trajectory of my life. In 1974, when I was fourteen, I found the Mettu Bethel Church, which had a Presbyterian background but at the time was completely Pentecostal in both teaching and practice. During a prayer meeting for young people, I received overwhelming power and the gift of speaking in tongues.

Eleven years later, while reading Galatians, I again felt overwhelming power rush through me when I realized that baptism is necessary for our salvation, unlike what I had been taught in the Pentecostal denomination. I was a twenty-five-year-old veterinary doctor, but since my experience in Mettu Illubabor all those years earlier, I had felt God calling me to ministry. This second experience compelled me to answer that calling. *It was that experience that led me into a detailed Bible study that in turn made me decide to be become a Lutheran. That day in 1985 I decided to join the seminary, which eventually led me to become a Lutheran pastor.*

In this book you will read that God gave the Holy Spirit to the church and that the Holy Spirit manifests Himself in Christian worship through gifts of grace. The book also tackles inaccurate interpretations about the gifts of grace, which were important to the Pentecostal and charismatic movements, and contends the Lutheran church should not neglect these gifts but rather encourage its members to practice them in worship. Scriptures regarding prophecy, tongues and their interpretation, and healings are studied in detail, exposing biblically incorrect practices by going back to the Greek, the language in which they were originally written. Specifically, I make a concerted effort to clarify the confusion surrounding the use of the gifts of grace in worship. For example, some say speaking in tongues in worship is desirable. Others say tongues are obsolete. Still others believe tongues are exclusively for personal prayer and do not belong in corporate worship. This book explains what the Scriptures teach on this and other gifts of grace.

As much as the arguments and recommendations in this book are helpful to readers in the context of Africa and especially Ethiopia, I strongly believe this book is beneficial for Western churches too. The world has become a small village because of the Internet and social media. Anything done in any corner of the world can be seen and heard at the other end of the world in seconds. Interpretations and practices of the gifts of grace, whether scripturally wrong or right, are accessible to everyone who has a smartphone.

Although the Ethiopian Evangelical Church Mekane Yesus (EEC-MY) is now the largest Lutheran denomination in the world, with eleven million members, the gifts of grace are also being practiced in the backyards of Western Christians through ethnic churches. The second generation born of immigrant parents is now on the move to start its own churches whose language of worship is English. These second-generation churches will be churches for everyone—blacks, whites, Asian Hispanics, and Native Americans. This book will be a helpful guide for not only these emerging churches but also neighboring Western churches.

This book came out of my personal struggles to understand the Scriptures and the differences between Pentecostal and Lutheran theology regarding the gifts of grace and the grace of God that has saved us. In these struggles I found my Lutheran charismatic identity. I wrote this book to help clergy and laity in the church study the Scriptures in depth before coming to conclusions or be swayed by teachings that may be or may not be supported by the Scriptures.

The book is an attempt to woo those who care about authentic interpretation of the Word to look once more at the text in its true meaning and context. It is also a challenge to those of us who take teachings, sermons, and dogmatic presentations for granted to evaluate whether what we believe and preach is really what God wants to communicate to His church.

It is my sincere prayer that fellow Christians will accept the teachings in this book as an aid to their Bible study and a tool for their daily lives. Through this book, I hope fellow ministers see that the gifts of grace are given to the church for the glory of God and for the further dissemination of the gospel in society, not to glorify people's egos or pump the desire of flesh. Above all, I pray that pastors, seminary teachers, students, evangelists, and church elders will use this material to teach their congregations and students and to clear up confusion about the interpretation and practice of the gifts of grace.

Chapter 1

A SHORT AUTOBIOGRAPHY

I grew up in a traditional Oromo family in southwestern Oromia in Illubabor Zone. Oromos are people of Cushitic and Hamitic descent. (Cush is Ham's son as mentioned in Genesis 9:2 and is also the proper name of Noah's grandson.) Oromos represent close to half the population of Ethiopia, which is estimated to be 120 million.

In the Oromo tradition, Waaqayyoo, the creator god, is worshiped, demons are feared, and ancestral spirits are sacrificed for. In this tradition, no sacrifice is ever offered to Waaqayyoo. He is beyond sacrifice. Rather, Waaqayyoo is to be honored as the creator and controller of the universe, a god in control of the smallest detail of life.

It was in September 1967, when I was seven years old, that I first heard the name of Jesus. My teacher, Seyoum Tesemma, proclaimed the gospel to all of us in government public school during a moral studies class. Seyoum was part of a small Presbyterian group that worshiped in the morgue of Mettu Hospital (now called Carl Hospital) in Mettu, the capital city of the former Illubabor province. I fell in love with the story of Israel crossing the Red Sea onto dry land with God's help and with all of the other Bible stories Seyoum shared with us. He proclaimed those who believe in Jesus Christ will have eternal life. He also taught us demons are liars and are powerless to those who believe in Jesus Christ.

Through *Seyoum's* testimony, I felt loved by God. I was no longer afraid of the demons my family dreaded. I started to testify to children my age in the village. In 1968, as my mother went to worship, the archdemon Kumho threatened to kill me in two years. My mom and our community feared the prophecy of Kumho would take place and I would die. (I obviously did not.) In 1969, two young men, Tadese Woldegiorgis and Shibiru, taught a summer Sunday School for the children of the village. It was then that I received a copy of the New Testament.

As a child, I walked from our village to Mettu to sell milk. One of my customers, Getachew Negatu, was impressed by my fifth-grade report card, and in 1972, when he learned that I walked seven kilometers to school, he invited me to live in his house. I got my first Bible from another person who lived in the same house as a present for teaching him how to read.

Encounter with the Charismatic Experience

The small group that gathered in the hospital morgue eventually called Pastor Kes Terfa Jarso from Goree, a town twenty kilometers south of Mettu. Fearing the Ethiopian Orthodox Tewahido Church, the state church that has persecuted Christians for decades, the governor personally gave Kes Terfa Jarso a plot of land. The group moved from the morgue to the pastor's living room, which he had built specifically for worship. There, I attended church for the first time ever in September 1974.

When I found Kes Terfa Jarso's church, it was attended by about thirty to fifty people, most of whom were young. The church was on fire with miracles of healing and exorcism. I saw the demons that had terrorized our family scream and leave people. I had read stories of exorcism in my New Testament and felt delighted I had found a power much stronger than the demons my family dreaded.

I started to attend a student gathering led by evangelist Kes Demie Wagari. At a late afternoon service on November 26, 1974, I experienced extraordinary power and joy accompanied with the reception of the gift of speaking in tongues. I didn't know what I was saying, but these tongues were accompanied by inexpressible joy that's hard to describe even now, decades later. After my charismatic experience, I read the whole Bible in three months. I was so hungry for the Word and learned the Old Testament stories in a short time.

Teenage Evangelist

At this time we had only one pastor and two evangelists for the whole province of Illubabor. The gospel was spreading like wildfire, with exorcisms and healings and other gifts of grace. But no one was trained to manage and lead the movement. So my friends and I started to preach with the little knowledge we had from reading the Bible. We told Bible stories about people being healed from diseases and about demons screaming and being exorcised.

In 1975, at an evening prayer meeting at Mr. Mekonnen's house in the village of Chabbaaqaa, a man brought his wife to us in the darkness of night after a demon had nearly driven her into the forest. She looked as though she was pregnant when we saw her in the dim lamplight. We started to pray, and the demon cried from within her and left. Her belly, which she said had been enlarged for two years and caused labor pains twice, shrank to a normal size. After this, the woman and her husband started to attend Mettu Bethel Church, which was about six kilometers from the village.

Another time, while I was praying in choir practice, I heard in my spirit that I should go to the village of Adiyya, which was ten kilometers south of Mettu. I invited my friend Kidane Bajiga to go with me, and we ran to the village, where I preached on Ezekiel 37 at a night prayer meeting attended by about twenty people. Demons were exorcised, and people received gifts, including speaking in tongues. The next morning, we were invited to a house where an elderly woman lived. This woman was paralyzed from the waist down and had not walked for twelve years. No one except the woman was in the house when we entered. We testified to the woman, and she received Jesus Christ as her Lord. Then Kidane and I lifted her up, brought her to the pillar at the center of the room that supported the hut, and helped her walk around the pillar while praying for her. It was the first time we had prayed for a lame person. Nothing happened. We took the woman to her bed and ran back to Mettu. A week later, when we returned to see if anything had happened, someone at the house told us the woman had gone to drink coffee with the neighbors. When she came back to greet us we saw she had shoes on and was able to walk.

It was this kind of work by young people that helped the Illubabor Bethel Synod grow to the size it is today. In fact, the synod now has two daughter synods (Jimma Bethel Synod and another synod in Teppii) and is organizing two more synods (one in Bedelle and one in Darimu). The places where we preached the gospel are now formally organized congregations, some of which have multiple daughter congregations. One such congregation is the Worqayii Dirree Mekane Yesus, which is 20 kilometers south of Mettu.

In those days the Mettu church did not have any choice other than to send youth like me to preach because there were no pastors or even evangelists. In September 1976, when I was only fifteen, the Mettu Bethel Church sent me to preach at Oddoo church, which was about twenty-five kilometers southwest of Mettu. The morning I preached, demons were exorcised from a woman named Ejigayehu, whom Alemu Sanbato and his wife, Fiqaadee, had brought to church for the first time that day. I had heard about Fiqaadee from our youth leader (and later pastor), Demie Wagari, and I went to Alemu and Fiqaadee's house later that day in Worqayii Dirree. The next Sunday six of us—me, Fiqadee Abbaa Qoroo, her husband Alemu Sanbatoo, and Ejigayehu and her husband Getachew Sanbato (who later became pastor of the Worqayii Dirree Mekane Yesus Bethel congregation)—started formal Sunday service at Worqayii Dirree. Seven congregations are now organized around this initial congregation, and it is one of the clusters of the Illubabor Bethel Synod of the EECMY.

I was a leader of the high school Christian fellowship group, training fellow students to become inductive Bible study leaders. I also joined the church choir, composing songs in the Amharic and Oromo languages and sometimes translating Amharic songs into the Oromo language. At university, I was a leader of the Ethiopian University Students' Christian Fellowship, the veterinary campus branch in Bishoftu. I graduated as a doctor of veterinary medicine (DVM) in 1985.

Following My Calling

The power that overwhelmed me in 1974 came with a call to ministry. I sensed deep in my soul that one day I must be a preacher of the gospel. But I suppressed this calling for a long time because of my love for science. Still, the calling followed me wherever I went.

I was assigned to Ambassel District of Wollo Administrative Region in northern Ethiopia as a provincial veterinary officer when I graduated from veterinary school. My friend Tsegaye Guracha and I were roommates in Dessie, the capital city of Wollo, which was 30 kilometers from Loga Haik, the town of my assignment.

One pleasantly breezy and sunny Saturday morning in 1985, I was sitting on a three-legged stool outside my residence, studying my Bible under the towering Tosa Mountain. As I read the book of Galatians, I was suddenly overwhelmed with warmth that went through my being.

> "For you are all sons of God through faith in Christ Jesus. For as many of you as were baptized into Christ have put on Christ. There is neither Jew nor Greek, there is neither slave nor free, there is neither male nor female; for you are all one in Christ Jesus. And if you are Christ's, then you are Abraham's seed, and heirs according to the promise" (Galatians 3:26-29).

When I read "for as many of you as were baptized into Christ have put on Christ," I understood in a different way than ever before what it means to "put on Christ." I realized baptism is necessary for our salvation. It is not something we do just to show that we believe in Christ. The Galatian text taught me we put on Christ, like a cloth, through baptism. It also explained that baptism along with faith is the foundation of Christian unity.

In that instant I understood not only baptism, but also the depth and meaning of the grace of God that had saved me. That was when I decided to join the seminary to learn more about what had just been revealed to me.

A short time later I was transferred to Assela Zonal Veterinary Laboratory as a junior research officer. Assela is 175 kilometers southeast of Finfinnee (Addis Ababa). It was while I was working in Assela that I married my longtime friend Tenagne Negussie Woldeyohannes. We were in Mettu congregation choir as teenagers. We didn't know we would end up marrying while we were singing together. Our wedding was on Saturday January 14, 1989. Our daughter Efrata was born the third quarter of the same year.

Looking for a way to put into practice what I had learned through my personal Bible study, I worked with three women and another man in 1989 to plant a Lutheran congregation in Assela affiliated with the EECMY. By 1991 we had forty people ready for adult confirmation class. The Central Ethiopia Synod, with its head office in Finfinnee, assigned Pastor Mezgebu Fufa to teach the class. By 1993 we had been officially accepted as a full-fledged congregation, with seventy-two communicant members. We elected our first council and hired an evangelist.

But for me this was not enough. My heart still burned with the call to ministry. After consulting with my wife, Tenagne Negussie (Tenusha), I joined the Mekane Yesus Seminary in September 1993. Our family income was slashed by Eth. Birr 1350.00, which at the time was a high monthly salary, equivalent to US$600. I am grateful to Tenusha and my daughter, Efrata, who bore with me the financial difficulty my decision caused our family.

I joined the seminary not only to answer the decades-old call to ministry I had received in 1974 but also to find a way to theologize my experiences in Mettu in 1974 and in Dessie in 1985. Accordingly, the paper for my bachelor's in theology was titled "The Controversy of Baptism: A Challenge to the EECMY." This paper was translated into Amharic as a booklet titled "Emnetachin Sifeten: Kidus Timket" ("When Our Faith is Challenged: Holy Baptism"). It was published by Yemisiratch Dimts, the publishing agency of the Mekane Yesus Church, and the church is still using it in confirmation class. As I write this, the church is translating the book into the Oromo language.

When I graduated from seminary in 1997, I was assigned to be assistant lecturer. By January 1998, the Ethiopian Graduate School of Theology had launched, and in 2000 I was one of the first students to graduate with a master's degree in systematic theology. My master's thesis was titled "The Charismatic Movement in the EECMY. Some Doctrinal and Practical Issues. An Explorative and Evaluative Case Study. The Case of the EECMY Congregations in Nekemte."

Relocating to the United States

In 1999 my wife was one of three people who represented African Lutherans at the United Nations meeting in New York. She applied for and was granted asylum, and my daughter and I followed in 2001, compelled to move to the United States for two reasons. First, my daughter was sick, and there was no medicine in Ethiopia that could treat her symptoms. (She recovered and has been well since.) The second reason was that at the time the government of Ethiopia was brutally persecuting Oromo intellectuals. I was a preacher in Oromo congregations of the Mekane Yesus Church in Finfinnee and freely spoke about the rights of people from the pulpit whenever the text took me there. But my wife was scared the security people would get me. In fact, a prominent Oromo pastor attending a service at Gullale Mekane Yesus Oromo Church told me a government security agent sat next to him one Sunday morning and said he had recorded the sermon I was preaching. The security agent said he could have incriminated me with the recording but that he would delete it because he liked that I was courageous in telling the truth.

In 2014 I earned a Master's of Sacred Theology (S.T.M) in societal theology from Lutheran Theological Seminary at Gettysburg (LTSG) in Pennsylvania. I was serving the Oromo Resurrection Evangelical Lutheran Church (ORELC) formerly Oromo Christian Fellowship (OCF) as its founding pastor for twelve years already. Charismatic experiences continued in a more challenging manner, as many of the people did not have proper doctrinal teachings about the sacraments. I continued to teach what I had learned through my formal seminary education and experience of planting churches in Assela despite challenges from brothers and sisters with Pentecostal background, some of whom were boldly teaching prosperity gospel.

Theologizing the Charismatic Experience with Conference Call Services

When COVID-19 hit in 2020, pastors didn't know how to keep their churches together. The government forbade public meetings, including Sunday worship. Individual Christians did not know how to react. I had to do something to bring tranquility and to guide the people to trust the Lord through the pandemic. So we started conference call services six days a week from 7 to 9 p.m.; on Sundays I would preach from the pulpit and broadcast the service on YouTube and Facebook. It was at this time I realized I could teach what I had learned in my lifetime about the charismatic movement while I had the attention of the people. What I taught at the Oromo Resurrection Evangelical Lutheran Church during COVID on our conference calls is the basis for the rest of this book.

Chapter 2

A LUTHERAN PERSPECTIVE ON THE CHARISMATIC MOVEMENT

The charismatic movement respects the dogma of the different churches in which it functions. It is not aimed at changing the dogma of the church to Pentecostal doctrine. God is using this movement to bring gifts that were deemed obsolete back to life and to energize church members to become powerful witnesses for Jesus. The charismatic movement is the testimony that the gospel of Jesus Christ never dies or gets old. It is evidence the gospel can roar back to life through the gifts of grace in God's timing.

It might be shocking for some to see "charismatic" and "Lutheran" in the same sentence. There are suggestions among Lutheran groups that the term "charismatic" means the intensification of natural talents, dynamic expressions of joy over the delivery from demonic powers or automatic responses of the subconscious, or ecstatic activities that primitive Christianity needed in order to win recognition but which we have learned to recognize as obsolete and possibly even pathological phenomena.[1]

The Lutheran Church—Missouri Synod (LCMS) has prayerfully studied this topic through its Commission on Theology and Church Relations (CTCR) and in April 1977 presented "The Lutheran Church and the Charismatic Movement: Guidelines for Congregations and Pastors." This helpful document provides guidelines for congregations and pastors. In the report the LCMS makes it clear "the church will accept with joy and gratitude any gift the Spirit in his grace may choose to bestow on us for the purpose of edifying the body of Christ. It will recognize that the Lord does not forsake his church but promises the abiding presence of his Spirit. The church, therefore, will not reject out of hand the possibility that God may in his grace and wisdom endow some in Christendom with the same abilities and powers he gave his church in past centuries. It will take care lest it quench the Spirit by failing to expect and pray for God's presence and power in building his church. But it will also take seriously the admonition of the apostle to 'test the spirits to see whether they are of God; for many false prophets have gone out into the world' (1 John 4:1; cf. 1 Corinthians 12:10). Above all, the church will not employ such gifts as though they were means of grace."[2]

It is commendable the LCMS has taken the issue seriously since the late 1960s, even assigning a committee to develop recommendations. Through the CTCR, the LCMS notes the following eight beliefs are dangerous to teach:

1. That God desires every Christian, following baptism, to have a "second experience" such as the "baptism with the Spirit."
2. That the so-called "gifts of the Spirit" are external signs by which we can assure ourselves that we have faith, are living in God's grace, or have the Spirit of God.

3. That God promises every Christian such gifts as speaking in tongues, healing, discerning of spirits, and prophecy and that God has given such a promise as a part of the "full" or complete gospel.
4. That a "conversion experience," "baptism with the Spirit," or other inner religious experience is necessary for, or should be urged upon, Christians in order that they may be certain either of having faith and salvation or of the indwelling of God's Spirit.
5. That a Christian who has not had such experience either has an incomplete faith, is unconverted and is still living under the rule of sin, or has only accepted Christ as his Savior but not as his Lord.
6. That the sanctification of a Christian is incomplete unless he possesses the gift of speaking in tongues.
7. That God promises healing and health to every Christian in this life and that, if such healing does not occur, it is due to a lack of faith.
8. That God gives guidance and leadership to the church today through visions and dreams or direct prophecy.[3]

The EECMY has similar consultation under the title "Theological Consultation on Charismatic Movement," which makes the following conclusions:

1. The EECMY recognizes charismatic experiences in its congregations as a blessing to the church if handled in the right way according to the Scriptures.
2. That there is a place for charismatic experience in Lutheran doctrine.
    a. That signs and wonders are scriptural and are attested in the Lutheran view if they are rightly performed based on the biblical truth.

b. That healing ministries presently conducted in many congregations of the church can be true manifestations of the Spirit.
c. The reality of four dimensions of healing has been noted in the presentation of Dr. A. Nordlander.

4. Spiritual healing, which is the restoration of broken fellowship between God and man.
5. Physical healing, which is restoring physical health.
6. Healing as deliverance and exorcism from Satan and evil spirits.
7. Social healing of broken relationships between human beings.[4]

Dr.Agne Nordlander in his presentation to the consultation on Charismatic Movement in the Mekane Yesus Church in 1993 notes that while Lutherans recognize we receive the Holy Spirit at baptism, it is also evident believers experience the infilling of the Holy Spirit, which is spiritual renewal (Acts 2:4; Acts 4:31; Acts 9:17). He also notes the reality and authenticity of the gifts of the Spirit practiced in the EECMY congregations and the danger of their misuse, as well as the distinction in doctrine and practice of the Holy Spirit between the Pentecostal movement and charismatic renewal.

Based on the above conclusions, the EECMY makes the following recommendations:

1. Ways of worship should not be considered dogma. There should be varieties in ways of worship with proper order. These should be contextualized according to the need of congregations. It is not necessary that human traditions or rites or ceremonies instituted by men should everywhere be the same (Augsburg Confession, Article 7).

2. The doctrine of the EECMY, such as the law and gospel, the distinction between theology of the cross and theology of glory, and the Sacraments (baptism and Holy Communion), is designed to enrich and strengthen the experience of charismatic renewal. It also recommended that the doctrine of the Holy Spirit be elaborated in teaching to all EECMY members on the basis of the Augsburg Confession, Article 3, in congregational teachings.[5]

While some gifts are completely gone from use in the Western world, in churches like the EECMY it is utterly undeniable that God's hand is moving, freeing people who are oppressed by witchcraft and healing the lame, the sick, and the disabled. I myself have been a witness to many healings, including seeing a middle-aged lame man walk after prayer. I also witnessed and performed many exorcisms myself in the villages of Illubabor. Our pastor, the Rev. Terfa Jarso, used to go from bed to bed testifying to patients in Mettu Hospital and exorcising demons wherever appropriate.

In a study I did in 2000 for my master's degree of theology at the Ethiopian Graduate School of Theology in Addis Ababa among Central Synod Nekemte area ministers, I found there are three ways to view the charismatic movement: evangelical Baptist, Pentecostal, and Lutheran. Among the pioneers,[6] 25% have an evangelical Baptist view of baptism in the Holy Spirit, 50% have a Pentecostal understanding, and 25% have a Lutheran understanding.[7] Among Mekane Yesus theologians in the Central Synod, including pastors, 59% have a Lutheran understanding of baptism in the Holy Spirit, 9% have an evangelical Baptist understanding, and 32% have a Pentecostal view. Of lay ministers and Bible school graduates, 42% have an evangelical Baptist view, 37% have a Pentecostal view, and 21% have a Lutheran understanding. Of ordinary members, 60% have a Pentecostal understanding, 30% have a Lutheran understanding, and 10% have an evangelical Baptist understanding.[8]

When we look at this statistics, we realize the EECMY has a lot to do to bring its pastors, evangelists, lay ministers, and members to the right understanding of Holy Baptism. It is alarming this many members of a Lutheran church believe baptism in the Spirit is a second blessing (in other words, they believe Christians need a second blessing, or baptism, of the Holy Spirit). This can cause contempt and division among members and ministers. Above all it is a wrong understanding of holy baptism.

The Catholic Church precedes the Lutheran church in its involvement in the charismatic movement. The charismatic movement began in the Catholic Church in 1967[9] and more easily disseminated among Catholics than Lutherans, as Catholics involved in the Pentecostal movement did not have difficulty with the doctrine of second blessing. They didn't debate how to systematize the experience that Pentecostals call baptism into the doctrine of the Catholic Church. In fact, they even used the designation "Catholic Pentecostals."[10]

Charismatics who have an evangelical Baptist view believe initiation takes place in one stage—in other words, they believe the Holy Spirit is given at regeneration when someone is born again, as specified in the *Dictionary of the Pentecostal and Charismatic Movements.*[11] They do not believe in a second initiation, or blessing. Charismatics who have a Lutheran view also believe there is only one initiation. They believe the substance of Holy Baptism in the Spirit is the reception of the Holy Spirit and forgiveness of sins. They differ from Baptists, though, in their belief in infant baptism and the sacramental value of Holy Baptism.

Pentecostals, on the other hand, believe in two-stage initiation, or second blessing. They believe that people are baptized in the Holy Spirit as a necessary second stage initiation, which happens subsequently and separately from regeneration. A segment of this group believes all Christians should speak in tongues and assumes those who do not speak in tongues have a spiritual problem that prevents them from being "baptized in the Holy Spirit." Non-Baptist Pentecostals believe in two-stage initiation of the reception of the Holy Spirit but believe that baptism, including infant baptism, is a means of grace. This group includes most people who consider themselves charismatic as members of Catholic and Lutheran churches, including the EECMY. There are Baptist Pentecostals and non-Baptist Pentecostals. Baptist Pentecostals believe that fullness or baptism in the Holy Spirit is a second initiation for the empowerment for ministry. They reject what we call holy baptism has any sacramental value. They call it water baptism even though that phrase doesn't exist in the Bible. They consider it as a testimony to the world that one has believed in Jesus Christ. Again this notion does not have any biblical support. The Scriptures they quote to support their claim, Romans 10:8-10 never mentions baptism.

In the Mekane Yesus church some people think they are Lutherans if they believe in infant baptism. These people are actually non-Baptist Pentecostals. We cannot call them Lutherans because they do not believe God baptizes people with the Holy Spirit during Holy Baptism, or they think that what happens during Holy Baptism is inadequate. Lutherans, on the other hand, believe the gift of the Holy Spirit is given at the moment of baptism as happened in Ephesus (Acts 19) and Caesarea (Acts 10), where those who were baptized spoke in tongues. Charismatic Lutherans believe the gifts of grace express themselves as baptized infants mature physically, psychologically and spiritually through family and Sunday school nurturing in biblical knowledge and spiritual journey. The difference with Pentecostals is that charismatic Lutherans demand that all charismatic gifts should be practiced according to the Scriptures (1 Corinthians 14:26-33). Those who are called to preach and teach must study the Bible in order to express themselves well and in an organized manner. Those who are given other gifts should also study the Scriptures and pray so they use their gifts in the right way.

Charismatic Lutherans believe the gift of tongues is beneficial when tongues are spoken in personal private prayer or silently spoken without disrupting the flow of a congregation's corporate worship service. They believe that when tongues are publicly spoken in the congregation without being interpreted, they are meaningless and disruptive. But if tongues are spoken in public worship and interpreted in a language the people understand, they become a message just like sermons, teachings, and prophecy.

We can contend the apostle Paul was a charismatic Lutheran because his arguments are identical to the arguments of charismatic Lutherans. Here are some texts that speak of Paul's experiences:

> "And Ananias went his way and entered the house; and laying his hands on him he said, 'Brother Saul, the Lord Jesus, who appeared to you on the road as you came, has sent me that you may receive your sight and be filled with the Holy Spirit.' Immediately there fell from his eyes something like scales, and he received his sight at once; and he arose and was baptized" (Acts 9:17-18).

> "Then he said, 'The God of our fathers has chosen you that you should know His will, and see the Just One, and hear the voice of His mouth. For you will be His witness to all men of what you have seen and heard. And now why are you waiting? Arise and be baptized, and wash away your sins, calling on the name of the Lord'" (Acts 22:14-16).

Paul was baptized by the Holy Spirit at the time of his baptism and wrote about how to use charismatic gifts in both private and corporate worship. Therefore, even though the terms "charismatic" and "Lutheran" were not used in Paul's time, people who call themselves charismatic Lutherans share Paul's understanding of the use of charismatic gifts. Hence, charismatic Lutherans are Pauline in their understanding, and Paul was charismatic Lutheran in his understanding.

I write this in the hope we will achieve the charismatic Lutheran worship as described in 1 Corinthians 12 and 14; Romans 12; Colossians 3:15-16; and Ephesians 4:9-13 and that in our worship services the gifts of grace, including tongues (with interpretation when done in corporate service), may be practiced according to the prescriptions in 1 Corinthians 14:26-33. But before we see how the gifts of grace function in the Lutheran service, I would like to look at the history of the charismatic movement.

Chapter 3

THE HISTORY OF THE CHARISMATIC MOVEMENT

The Christian church was charismatic at its very inception. Jesus preached the kingdom of God. He healed the sick and exorcised demons. The apostles did the same. The five hundred disciples potentially present in Jerusalem on the day of Pentecost spoke in the different languages of the Diaspora Jews who were in the city that day. The book of Acts is full of miracles God did through the ministry of Paul and Peter. For example, Peter and John healed a paralytic at the gate of the temple in Acts 3, and Acts 9 speaks of the restoration of Dorcas and the healing of Aeneas.

The Reformation

After the Apostolic Age, the church of Christ drifted away from the Scriptures, focusing instead on traditions. God used Martin Luther and his friends to bring the church back to the Scriptures. The Reformation revealed the grace of God that saves sinners and brought to light the understanding that none are saved by works of righteousness. It coined the "solas": sola gratia (grace alone), sola fide (faith alone), sola Scriptura (Scripture alone), sola Christos (Christ alone), and soli Deo gloria (glory to God alone). Through these phrases Luther turned the attention of the common Christian from tradition and the power of the papacy to faith in Jesus Christ and the study of the Scriptures.

But after the Reformation the church regressed to sterile orthodoxy, where the Scriptures were pushed to the periphery of the Christian experience. Philipp Jakob Spener, who is regarded as the father of pietism, reacted against this orthodoxy among the immoral and the terrible social conditions following the Thirty Years' War (1618-48). Spener advocated for intensive Bible study individually and in *collegia pietatis* (groups of Christians meeting to study the Scriptures and devotional literature). These pietistic groups were called *ecclesiolae in ecclesia,* which in Latin means "little churches within the church." Spener also encouraged the universal priesthood of believers through increased lay activity. He taught the practice of Christianity in daily life and works of unselfish love. He advocated dealing with believers and heretics with sincere prayers, good example, persuasive dialogue, and the spirit of love instead of compulsion.[12]

The Encyclopedia of the Lutheran Church claims that "pietism is the grandest and strongest attempt ever made in the church to restore present-day Christianity to its original stature"[13] next to the Reformation. One of the leaders of the pietistic movement, August Hermann Francke, insisted the necessary reformation of doctrine by Luther must lead to a reformation of life. Francke believed he was entirely Lutheran in asserting that faith must become active in love. Spener and Francke remained lifelong Lutherans, saying regeneration was an integral part of an experience of justification.[14]

Spener and Francke attempted to walk the middle ground between dogmatic rigidity and emotional warmth, between faith and works, between justification and sanctification, and between forsaking the fallen world and affirming it through love of neighbor, enemies, and God's creation.[15] Pietism, with its emphasis on group study of the Scriptures and putting faith into practice while still promoting Lutheran doctrine, can be considered the first step toward what has become charismatic Lutheranism. The Puritans of the sixteenth and seventeenth centuries also wrote about the ways God's grace could work in human experience, penetrating through formal religion to an inner transformation from death and sin to life in Christ.[16]

The Great Awakening and the Christian Missions

Through the ministry of Jonathan Edwards and George Whitefield in the early eighteenth century a great religious awakening swept through America. This evangelical movement left a permanent impact on American Protestantism. No longer would Christianity be dominated by ritual, ceremony, and hierarchy; instead it would become a much more personal religion. It gave average people the means to develop an individual sense of spiritual conviction and encouraged men and women across the colonies to study their own relationships with God and commit to a new standard of Christian morality. Preachers traveled great distances to spread their evangelical message and to be heard by new audiences.[17]

Christian missions owe a lot to the evangelical revival. Anglican piety, mystical tradition, and pietism combined to produce John Wesley and the Methodist movement in Britain. Protestant Christians were mostly unable or unwilling themselves to take up the cause of missions. Therefore, the work was left to individuals motivated by the Spirit to lead the movement depending on financial contributions of interested Christians.[18]

English Baptists were the pioneers (1792), followed by the London Missionary Society (1795), with its laudable aim of preaching the gospel to the heathen. As a result, the gospel spread to Asia and Africa, motivating the English missionary pioneer William Carey (1761-1834) to propose a general missionary conference, which was held in 1810 at the Cape of Good Hope.

Edward Smither reports the church in Africa grew from ten million believers in 1910 to nearly four hundred million in 2010.[19] Debela Birri in his book *Divine Plan Unfolding: The Story of Ethiopian Evangelical Church Bethel* discusses the accomplishments of the missionary societies as they reached the Oromo people who lived in the land now included in the territory of Ethiopia with the gospel of Jesus Christ.[20] The German Hermannsburg Mission (GHM), the Swedish Evangelical Mission (SEM), and the Presbyterian Church USA reached Wollega and Illubabor in western Oromia in present-day Ethiopia in the early twentieth century.

In *Evangelical Pioneers in Ethiopia: The Origins of the Evangelical Church Mekane Yesus*, Gustav Aren details the early endeavors of evangelical Christians to reform the Ethiopian Orthodox Tewahido Church until the SEM and GHM started evangelical movement among the Oromos in the 1900s in Ethiopia.[21] Through this missionary movement, the gospel traveled across the globe to people never before included in the church. The Holy Spirit motivated leaders of the missionary movement to plant churches in unreached parts of the world on the foundation the apostles had laid. That same Spirit quickened the church through the Pentecostal and Charismatic movements to return to its God-intended sense of a joyful personal relationship with God and deep care for people unreached by the gospel of Jesus Christ. The gifts of grace exhibited in the ministry of missionaries helped the gospel travel thousands of miles to people who had never heard about the love of God through the sacrifice of His Son, Jesus Christ.

The Pentecostal Movement and the Charismatic Renewal

The Pentecostal movement proclaims that the spiritual power of the first-century church can be the norm for the church today. It began on January 1, 1901, at Charles F. Parham's Bethel Bible School in Topeka, Kansas, with the identification of speaking in tongues as the evidence of baptism in the Holy Spirit. The movement was promoted by William J. Seymour, a black Holiness preacher, at a revival at the Azusa Street Mission (1906-1909) in Los Angeles.[22] As the movement spread across denominations, it took its name from the word charisma, which Paul had referred to as "gifts of grace." It has since become one of the most significant forces of church growth. In 1975 University of Chicago historian Martin Marty reported some observers had identified the Pentecostal/charismatic movement as the "first force" in the Christian world, "while the more staid counterparts foundered or remained static."[23]

The charismatic movement refers to the use of the gifts of grace in Christian worship service. Charisma (Χαρισμα) is a verbal noun of χαριζομαι[24] ("gifts of grace").[25] Χαρισμα is grace the spiritual manifestations are called χαρισματα ("gifts of grace"). In 1 Corinthians 12-14 and Romans 12 the ecstatic phenomena at divine worship, which are regarded as operations of the Spirit—notably, speaking in tongues and prophecy—are described as χαρισματα.[26] For Paul Χαρισμα ("gifts of grace") is similar to πνευμα "(the Spirit") and πνευματικα. Χαρισμα is given to people at baptism or at the proclamation of the gospel.[27] These gifts express themselves as the Christian matures in faith in the Christian journey. But this does not mean that God does not give the gifts of grace to immature Christians. That is what we learn in the experience of the Corinthian Church.

The charismatic renewal initiated a new dimension of Christian living, with far-reaching consequences for most aspects of the Christian life.[28] Peter Hocken, in the *Dictionary of Pentecostal and Charismatic Movements*, writes that the first characteristic of this movement is a focus on Jesus. In this regard the witness to the experience of reception of power and gifts of grace refers to an encounter with Jesus, a deeper yielding to Jesus, and a fuller acceptance of Jesus as Lord.[29] The proclamation "Jesus is Lord!" is, in fact, the slogan of the charismatic renewal. Jesus is known as the living Lord at the heart of Christian worship—the Lord who speaks in the present, delivers people from evil, and heals the sick.

The second characteristic of charismatic renewal is praise, evoked by the coming of the Holy Spirit to the believer. As a result, the believer has a new capacity to give glory to God, which is evident in the spontaneity of charismatic praise and symbolized by the gift of tongues.

A great love and thirst for Scripture, which has consistently marked the charismatic renewal, is the third characteristic of the movement. Charismatics believe God speaks both individually and corporately today, just as He did in the first century.

Additional characteristics of the movement include a new capacity and freedom to speak freely to others about the Lord and an awareness of the reality of Satan and the powers of evil, which means an increased focus on deliverance and exorcism. Charismatic renewal is also accompanied by an increased expectancy and longing for the return of Christ (παρουσια).[30]

Brian Fargher, a former missionary of the Sudan Interior Mission, observes five distinguishing features of the movement in Ethiopia:

1. An emphasis upon the literal meaning of the Bible.
2. An increase in congregational participation. Women and youth started to participate more in preaching and prayer. The movement's leaders introduced an inductive Bible study group, where the norm was participatory discussion.
3. A new emphasis on prayer, purity, and propagation. People started to expect great things from God through fervent prayer.
4. Speaking in tongues, which was wrongly considered to be a necessity for all Christians at the beginning of the movement.
5. The belief that "baptism of the Spirit," accompanied by tongue speaking, imparts to the recipient a type of perfection.[31] This belief offended people who were unsympathetic initially.

> Worse, some people taught that those who did not speak in tongues must have unconfessed sins or that they were still continuing in sinful lives. This attitude hurt many Christians who were given charismatic gifts other than speaking in tongues.

Fargher also notes many new hymns were composed in charismatic circles. In fact, repetition of the choruses of these hymns is one of the characteristics of charismatic worship.[32] As worshipers repeat the choruses, they have time to meditate on the meaning of the words, which brings them into a state of joy, sorrow over their sins, or confidence in the Lord. Emotion, too, is involved in charismatic worship: Worshipers feel unusually pleasant feelings when they sense the Holy Spirit moving.

Fargher further expresses the importance of music in the charismatic movement:

> "The renewal movement brought a powerful new figure into Ethiopian church history: the soloist.[33] Many of these men and women were able to make whole congregations dissolve into tears or shout out 'halleluiahs' and 'Amens.'... The introduction of Chorus singing has enabled the whole congregation to share in music in a way which was previously impossible. People participated in singing, in prayer, in giving testimony, in prophecy, in speaking in tongues, and interpreting the tongues. In doing so many unlearned people got the chance to participate in the worship which in turn made the worship more meaningful to the worshipers.[34]

The impact of the Pentecostal and charismatic movements has changed the face of Christianity around the world and ushered in a new era of Christian spirituality.[35] The charismatic renewal represents a transdenominational movement of Christians who emphasize a life in the Spirit and the importance of exercising extraordinary gifts of the Spirit, including but not limited to speaking in tongues in private prayer and public worship. Charismatics have tended to recognize the ebb and flow of fervent spirituality in Christian history and have found their identity as part of the latest wave of renewal.[36] The charismatic renewal understands itself as a renewal of biblical faith and experience.[37] This has never become a breakaway movement. It generally has remained in its mother churches.

The movement is theologically diverse but generally orthodox. Charismatics believe that today God gives the gifts of the grace explained in the Bible to be used personally and corporately in the life of the church. The movement is evangelistic in nature and reformist **supporting or advancing gradual reform** in character, with a tendency to depart from the sectarianism usually associated with most Pentecostal movements. This is a significant difference from Pentecostalism.[38]

The Classical Pentecostal View of the Charismatic Experience

Classical Pentecostalism arose from Baptist bodies and Holiness groups that were reacting against the secularism and rationalism then seemingly dominant in the institutional churches.[39] Pentecostal denominations stressed an experience called the "baptism in the Holy Spirit" as a second stage after conversion or as a third stage after both conversion and sanctification in the life of the believer. The evidence of this experience was assumed to be speaking in tongues [40] These denominations, however, did not believe baptism in the Holy Spirit was essential for salvation. Instead, they followed the two-stage view of Christian initiation.

The two-stage view holds that salvation, conversion, or acceptance of Christ as Lord and Savior is separate from and prior to the experience of baptism in the Holy Spirit. Proponents say every Christian should be baptized in the Spirit and should exhibit this by speaking in tongues. According to the classical Pentecostal view, Christians who do not experience this, though they are saved, lack the baptism in the Spirit that gives power for prayer and evangelism.[41]

Classical Pentecostals, like charismatics, deny the cessation of teaching that has been the standard understanding of the Western churches since the days of Saint Augustine. The rise of classical Pentecostalism, therefore, forced the church to reexamine the position that the χαρισματα ("gifts of grace") had ceased in light of the many claims made for current manifestations of the charismatic gifts.[42]

Most classical Pentecostal groups adhere to the doctrine that speaking in tongues is a personal experience that certifies the baptism of the Holy Spirit. But many classical Pentecostals admit the doctrine of speaking in tongues as initial evidence of the baptism of the Holy Spirit cannot be proved from 1 Corinthians. The doctrine finds its sole support from the historical precedent of the cases of the Spirit's descent in Acts 2; Acts 10; and Acts 19.[43]

This Pentecostal error is one brick on top of the error of the Baptists. The Baptists claim verbal pronouncement of faith in Jesus Christ precedes Holy Baptism, effectively excluding children of Christian families from the kingdom of God. Baptists wrongly interpret Mark 16:16 in claiming that faith precedes baptism; rather, the text is two complete sentences tied together by the conjunction "and" to signify the importance of both baptism and faith for salvation. Paul teaches in Romans 10:17 that "faith comes by hearing, and hearing by the word of God." Children of Christian families should be baptized and taught the word of God in order for them to believe instead of being excluded from the family of believers. The argument Baptists and Pentecostals make is unprecedented in the Old Testament, for children born in a Jewish family are included in the family of faith through circumcision (Genesis 17:9ff). Baptists exclude children from the means of grace namely the forgiveness of their inherited sins. Pentecostals believe the error of Baptists and add to it. They believe that those Christians that don't speak in tongues or don't have a second initiation, they call baptism in the Spirit, are denied this second experience because of a sinful life or unforgiven sins. By doing this they create a second class of Christians causing haughtiness on those who have the gift of speaking in tongues and sorrow and blame on those who don't speak in tongues.

Back to the Charismatic Doctrine and Experience of the Early Church

From its inception the church has ministered by the gifts of grace. There has never been a service without preaching, teaching, singing, and other gifts of the Spirit. This is because the very presence of the Holy Spirit necessitates charismatic gifts, as these gifts are given by the Holy Spirit Himself.

With the arrival of the Pentecostal movement, the gift of tongues and its interpretation reappeared in some services, and the movement revitalized praise and enthusiasm for testifying to the good news of Jesus Christ. But despite its immense benefits, this movement had a fundamental defect. The problem with the Pentecostal movement was—and still is—that it makes the gift of tongues a universal necessity for all Christians, as many Pentecostals believe speaking in tongues is the sign of the filling, or the baptism, of the Holy Spirit. This has divided the church into two—those baptized by the Holy Spirit and those not baptized by the Holy Spirit—based on their ability to speak in tongues.

Those who speak in tongues are considered baptized by the Holy Spirit and obedient to God. It's assumed, if not taught, that those who do not speak in tongues have spiritual problems. I have seen many who fast and pray and wonder why they are not baptized by the Holy Spirit while their friends receive the gift of tongues and consider themselves baptized. This comes from misunderstanding the fact that God gives different gifts of grace to everyone as He wills. It also comes from wrongly understanding that speaking in tongues is universal to all Christians.

The teaching of charismatic gifts is not new. It is not a Pentecostal movement in mainline churches. Rather, *the teaching of the gifts of grace is biblical and non-Pentecostal*. The correct understanding of the doctrine of the gifts of grace comes full circle to Paul's teaching in his epistles (Romans 12:9ff; 1 Corinthians 12; 1 Corinthians 14; Ephesians 4; Colossians 3:16-17). The Pentecostal doctrine is erroneous and non-biblical when it makes speaking in tongues a universal necessity and a sign of being filled by the Holy Spirit. This doctrine is harmful both to those who receive the gift of tongues and to those who do not, for it makes the former haughty and the latter self-blaming.

The Future in Perspective

In 2021 Lifeway Research published some startling statistics: "In 2019, approximately 3,000 Protestant churches were started in the U.S., but 4,500 Protestant churches closed, according to estimates from Nashville-based Lifeway Research. The evangelical research organization analyzed congregational information from 34 denominations and groups representing 60% of U.S. Protestant churches to arrive at the church plant and closure numbers for 2019. The current closure gap indicates a shift from Lifeway Research's previous analysis. For 2014, an estimated 4,000 Protestant churches were planted, while 3,700 closed in a year."[44]

More churches closed than opened in 2019. Then came the pandemic. Losses have denominations focused on church planting and revitalization, but it's been a challenge.

Philip Jenkins states that "the church of the future will be the church of South America, the church of Africa, the church of China and Japan. Christianity is moving decisively to the Global South: the domain of the charismatic movement." In 2025 the title for the "most Christian" continent will be a competition between Africa and Latin America, he says, writing that "there is no doubt that in 2050 Africa will win. In terms of population distribution Christianity will be chiefly a religion of Africa and the African diaspora, which will, in a sense, be the heartland of Christianity." By 2050, he writes, "At the head of the list will still be Europe, followed in no particular order by Brazil,

Mexico, Nigeria, the Congo, Ethiopia, the Philippines, and China."[45] This means that Europe will have the highest raw numbers of Christians, but Africa will be the continent where Christians make up the biggest percentage of the population.

On April 4, 2019, the Lutheran World Federation reported the EECMY was a church of 9.3 million people. The church now reports it has exceeded ten million baptized members, and it's still growing. The problem is the kind of Christianity that's being preached there. A September 2019 article from the *Ethiopia Observer* notes:

> "A group of self-proclaimed 'apostles' and 'prophets' are commanding some of the country's largest spiritual audiences through pulpits and television cameras. They, among others, promise direct access to God through miracles and healing and give assurance of prosperity and abundance. Ministries like Tamrat Tarekegn, Eyu Chufa, Yontan Aklilu, Jeremiah Hussen, Tibebu Workeye, and Birtukan Tassew claim millions of followers and their brand of prosperity gospel is winning the public's hearts and minds. In stark contrast to traditional Charismatic churches such as Mekane Yesus, Meserete Krestos [a Mennonite-turned-Pentecostal church], Qale Heywet [a Baptist-turned-Pentecostal church], and Mulu Wongel, the new breed of preachers use a multi-level marketing system to sell faith and optimism to connect directly with millions of customers, allowing them to reap millions in donations. Yet, the often-aggressive strategy in compelling believers to show their faith through payments, which they say will be recompensed in the form of wealth makes many wary. Some accuse them of being motivated by pure greed and exploiting the poor and the miserable."[46]

The politics of Ethiopia is led by Prime Minister Abiy Ahmed, a follower of prosperity gospel. Even the name of his party is Prosperity Party. *Ethiopia Insight* wrote in April 2021 that "Abiy's leadership style is embedded in the ethos of these prosperity gospel philosophies."[47] Mekane Yesus pastors are not equipped to confront the heresy behind prosperity gospel. The prosperity gospel will be detrimental for Mekane Yesus's own members in Ethiopia. But the danger is not limited to Ethiopia; this kind of Christianity will be disseminated from its new center of gravity, the Global South, which includes Ethiopia to Europe, and the United States and Canada through the diaspora. The reasons for growth in the Global South are well reported by Jenkins. These include decline in the West, the types of Christianity in the Global South, and the prosperity gospel coming back to roost in America where it was originated.

Weakness in the West and the power by which false Christianity comes from the South are devastating for what is left of the Western church. From a human perspective, it is very difficult to defend the truth. Cult worship that defies reason and scriptures like the QAnon are flourishing in America even though it takes detailed research to find out why people turn to cult and personality worship. Cult worship has become a breeding ground for false Christianity in America. It is crucial we equip pastors in the Global South with sound doctrine to help them fight heresy in their churches so this distorted version of Christianity will not come back to ruin the Christian faith in the West.

Jenkins writes that "the process of Christian expansion outside Europe and the West does seem inevitable." He explains the reasons:

1. Decline in the proportion of the world's people who live in the traditionally advanced nations.
2. Increase of population growth rates in the South.[48]

Jenkins even contends the growth of the church in the South has affected the mixture of Christians in the West. He explains that half the congregations in the Boston-Cambridge area worship in languages other than English.[49] The Greater Boston Baptist Association at one time used posters on subway trains to spread its evangelistic message in English, French, Spanish, Portuguese, and Korean. In addition, the arrival of black people from the Caribbean and Africa has necessitated a new wave of black churches, and the arrival of Latinos in high numbers has altered the nature of U.S. Catholicism.[50] The presence of immigrant Christians with different religious worship expressions is likely to introduce the practices of newer churches into the religious mainstream of the host nations both in Europe and America.[51]

In a section titled "Evangelizing the North," Jenkins argues that "about one-sixth of the priests currently serving in American parishes [in the Catholic Church] have been imported from other countries, African priests appearing in—of all places—Ireland, that ancient nursery of Catholic devotion.[52] Great Britain has some 1,500 missionaries from fifty nations. Many come from African countries, and they express disbelief at the spiritual desert they encounter."[53]

Let me wind up this discussion with what CNN reported on Easter 2023. CNN's report quoted Tish Harrison Warren, a *New York Times* columnist, who had written: "The future of American Christianity is neither white evangelicalism nor white progressivism. The future of American Christianity now appears to be a multiethnic community that is largely led by immigrants of or [not of] the children of immigrants." CNN's report went on to say, "If the American church can embrace this future and reverse its shrinking membership, it will have experienced its own resurrection."[54]

Chapter 4

THE PERSON AND ATTRIBUTES OF THE HOLY SPIRIT

The charismatic experience is not foreign to the Scriptures. Rather, it is explained in the Scriptures. The Scriptures assume that discipleship, mission, and every worship activity is done by the gifts of grace, as teaching, preaching, prayer, singing, and other gifts are practiced in all worship services. But before we explain how the gifts of grace work in the worship service in the Christian church, we will look at the person and attributes of the Holy Spirit, who is the giver of these gifts.

The Person of the Holy Spirit

The Holy Spirit is referred to as a person in the Holy Scriptures. The authors of the Scriptures refer to the Holy Spirit with a definite article every time, beginning in Genesis 1:2. Jesus calls the Holy Spirit "another Helper" in John 14:16 and "the Spirit" in the following verse. Just like Jesus said, "I am the way, the truth, and the life," the Holy Spirit is the Spirit of truth—the Spirit of truth that the world cannot receive because it cannot see Him or know Him. But the church knows Him.

There are many more texts that support the personhood of the Holy Spirit. My intention is that we remember from the get-go that the Holy Spirit is not just a power or a wind that comes to do something on demand or whenever the Father sends Him. The teaching of the personhood of the Holy Spirit is not the creation of the church but is rather the church's recognition of His personhood as recorded in the Scriptures. He is the third person of the Trinity. The Lutheran church begins its service in the name of the Father and of the Son and of the Holy Spirit, recognizing the personhood of all three persons in one Godhead.

The Holy Spirit is God. All divine attributes are ascribed to Him. The apostle Peter calls the Holy Spirit God (Acts 5:3-4). Here is the text (emphasis mine):

"But Peter said, 'Ananias, why has Satan filled your heart to *lie to the Holy Spirit* and keep back part of the price of the land for yourself? While it remained, was it not your own? And after it was sold, was it not in your own control? Why have you conceived this thing in your heart? You have not lied to men but to God.'"

In this text the apostle Peter confirms that lying to the Holy Spirit is lying to God. Therefore, Ananias and Sapphira received a punishment for lying to the Holy Spirit.

The Holy Spirit is omnipresent (present at all places in one time). This quotation from Psalm 139:7-12 proves the Spirit of God is present in all places and that there is no way to escape from His presence: "Where can I go from Your Spirit? Or where can I flee from Your presence? If I ascend into heaven, You are there; If I make my bed in hell, behold, You are there. If I take the wings of the morning, And dwell in the uttermost parts of the sea, Even there Your hand shall lead me, And Your right hand shall hold me. If I say, 'Surely the darkness shall fall on me,' Even the night shall be light about me; Indeed, the darkness shall not hide from You, But the night shines as the day; The darkness and the light are both alike to You."

The Holy Spirit is omniscient (knows everything). Just like God the Father and God the Son, God the Holy Spirit knows all things. In 1 Corinthians 2:9-10, Paul writes (emphasis mine): "'Eye has not seen, nor ear heard, Nor have entered into the heart of man. The things which God has prepared for those who love Him.' But God has revealed them to us through His Spirit. *For the Spirit searches all things, yes, the deep things of God.*" Paul says he speaks the wisdom of God in a mystery because he is instructed by the Holy Spirit, who searches all things, including the deep things of God.

The Holy Spirit is omnipotent (all powerful). Just as God the Father and God the Son are omnipotent, so is God the Holy Spirit. The psalmist sings, "You send forth Your Spirit, they are created; And You renew the face of the earth" (Psalm 104:30). The Holy Spirit has the power to create and renew the face of the earth. We read in Genesis 1:2 that creation is ascribed to Him: "The earth was without form, and void; and darkness was on the face of the deep. And the Spirit of God was hovering over the face of the waters." It was under the incubating wings of the Holy Spirit that the earth was formed and darkness gave way to light. The author of Hebrews writes that Jesus Christ our Lord offered Himself through the Holy Spirit, the "eternal Spirit" (Hebrews 9:14), and John writes that the Holy Spirit is worshiped (Revelation 1:4). We are baptized in the name of the Holy Spirit as well as in the name of the Father and the Son. It is the Holy Spirit who gives us Christian identity by indwelling us, as will be explained in future chapters.

The Holy Spirit as Explained in the Three Chief Creeds of the Christian Faith

The Apostles' Creed doesn't give much explanation about the Holy Spirit. Yet it states that Christians should confess, "I believe in the Holy Spirit," just as they confess, "I believe in God the Father" and "I believe in Jesus Christ, His only Son, our Lord."[55]

The Nicene Creed gives more details about the person of the Holy Spirit. Here, the Holy Spirit is called "the Lord and giver of life, who proceeds from the Father and the Son: who together with the Father and the Son is worshiped and glorified: who spoke by the prophets."[56] The part that explains the person of the Holy Spirit was the resolution of the Council of Constantinople in AD 381.

In the Athanasian Creed all three persons of the Godhead are explained in more detail. This creed states that the Holy Spirit should be understood without being divided from the divine substance as a separate person. The Holy Spirit is equal in glory and coequal in majesty, uncreated, unlimited, eternal, and almighty, the creed says. The Holy Spirit is God and Lord. He is not created, just as the Father and the Son are not created, and He proceeds from the Father and the Son. The Holy Spirit, along with the two other persons of the Trinity, is not before or after the other persons of the Trinity. Accordingly, the Athanasian Creed states that "all three persons are coequal and coeternal, and ... three persons are to be worshiped in one Godhead and one God is to be worshiped in three persons."[57]

The Holy Spirit Himself Is the Gift of God

The Holy Spirit Himself is the greatest gift: the gift of God. Just as Jesus Christ is the gift of God to the world, the Holy Spirit is the gift of God to those who believe in Jesus Christ. As it's written in John 3:16, "For God so loved the world that He gave His only begotten Son, that whoever believes in Him should not perish but have everlasting life." Jesus Christ was given so the world would believe in Him and receive forgiveness of sins through His sacrifice. John writes: "Nevertheless I tell you the truth. It is to your advantage that I go away; for if I do not go away, the Helper will not come to you; but if I depart, I will send Him to you. And when He has come, He will convict the world of sin, and of righteousness, and of judgment: of sin, because they do not believe in Me" (John 16:7-9).

Additional Scripture passages confirm the Holy Spirit is the gift of God. One is found in Peter's sermon on the day of Pentecost. "Then Peter said to them, 'Repent, and let every one of you be baptized in the name of Jesus Christ for the remission of sins; and you shall receive the gift of the Holy Spirit'" (Acts 2:38). In an effort to reason the workings of God in order to break new ground among the gentiles for the gospel of Jesus Christ, Peter explains: "And as I began to speak, the Holy Spirit fell upon them, as upon us at the beginning. Then I remembered the word of the Lord, how He said, 'John indeed baptized with water, but you shall be baptized with the Holy Spirit.' If therefore God gave them the same gift as He gave us when we believed on the Lord Jesus Christ, who was I that I could withstand God? When they heard these things they became silent; and they glorified God, saying, 'Then God has also granted to the Gentiles repentance to life'" (Acts 11:15-18).

Peter again testifies to the Jerusalem Council with similar words, saying, "So God, who knows the heart, acknowledged them by giving them the Holy Spirit, just as He did to us" (Acts 15:8). Peter gives yet another testimony to substantiate that the Holy Spirit is the gift of God: "The God of our fathers raised up Jesus whom you murdered by hanging on a tree. Him God has exalted to His right hand to be Prince and Savior, to give repentance to Israel and forgiveness of sins. And we are His witnesses to these things, and so also is the Holy Spirit whom God has given to those who obey Him" (Acts 5:30-32).

It is also written in Joel 2:28: "And it shall come to pass afterward That I will pour out My Spirit on all flesh; Your sons and your daughters shall prophesy, Your old men shall dream dreams, Your young men shall see visions." We have to make a distinction between the gift and the gifts. The gifts are given by the gift—the Holy Spirit—who is meant to be given in a certain age known in the mind of God (God's timing, or Kairos. These times are the last days, which started the day Jesus was born and will extend to His second coming (Galatians 4:4).

In his sermon in Acts 2:38, Peter does not speak about the gifts of the Holy Spirit. Instead, he speaks about the Holy Spirit as the gift. God gave the Holy Spirit to the church. The coming of the Holy Spirit required the birth, passion, death, and resurrection of Jesus Christ. This ushered in the church age.

John writes that Jesus said: "And these things I did not say to you at the beginning, because I was with you. But now I go away to Him who sent Me, and none of you asks Me, 'Where are You going?'" (John 16:4-5).

The Holy Spirit Is Not a Novice

To some people the Holy Spirit might seem to be a new member of the Trinity. But the Holy Spirit is revealed as Creator on the first pages of the Bible: "In the beginning God created the heavens and the earth. Now the earth was formless and empty, darkness was over the surface of the deep, and the Spirit of God was hovering over the waters" (Genesis 1:1-2). In another instance the Holy Spirit is described as the giver of wisdom, understanding in knowledge and in all manner of workmanship, as revealed to Moses. "Then the Lord spoke to Moses, saying: 'See, I have called by name Bezalel the son of Uri, the son of Hur, of the tribe of Judah. And I have filled him with *the Spirit of God*, in wisdom, in understanding, in knowledge, and in all manner of workmanship, to design artistic works, to work in gold, in silver, in bronze, in cutting jewels for setting, in carving wood, and to work in all manner of workmanship'" (Exodus 31:1-5, emphasis mine).

Even Pharaoh of Egypt recognized the Holy Spirit. "And Pharaoh said to his servants, 'Can we find such a one as this, a man in whom is the *Spirit of God*?' Then Pharaoh said to Joseph, 'Inasmuch as God has shown you all this, there is no one as discerning and wise as you. You shall be over my house, and all my people shall be ruled according to your word; only in regard to the throne will I be greater than you'" (Genesis 41:38-40, emphasis mine).

When Balaam wanted to curse Israel, the Holy Spirit blessed His people by the mouth of the diviner. "Now when Balaam saw that it pleased the Lord to bless Israel, he did not go as at other times, to seek to use sorcery, but he set his face toward the wilderness. And Balaam raised his eyes, and saw Israel encamped according to their tribes; and the Spirit of God came upon him. Then he took up his oracle and said: 'The utterance of Balaam the son of Beor, The utterance of the man whose eyes are opened, The utterance of him who hears the words of God, Who sees the vision of the Almighty, Who falls down, with eyes wide open: How lovely are your tents, O Jacob! Your dwellings, O Israel! Like valleys that stretch out, Like gardens by the riverside, Like aloes planted by the Lord, Like cedars beside the waters'" (Numbers 24:1-6).

The Holy Spirit gave words of prophecy to King Saul even before he was crowned. "'Then the Spirit of the Lord will come upon you, and you will prophesy with them and be turned into another man. And let it be, when these signs come to you, that you do as the occasion demands; for God is with you. You shall go down before me to Gilgal; and surely I will come down to you to offer burnt offerings and make sacrifices of peace offerings. Seven days you shall wait, till I come to you and show you what you should do.' So it was, when he had turned his back to go from Samuel, that God gave him another heart; and all those signs came to pass that day. When they came there to the hill, there was a group of prophets to meet him; then the Spirit of God came upon him, and he prophesied among them. And it happened, when all who knew him formerly saw that he indeed prophesied among the prophets, that the people said to one another, 'What is this that has come upon the son of Kish? Is Saul also among the prophets?'" (1 Samuel 10:6-11).

The Holy Spirit also came upon David as Samuel the prophet anointed him with olive oil. "Samuel said to Jesse, 'Are all the young men here?' Then he said, 'There remains yet the youngest, and there he is, keeping the sheep.' And Samuel said to Jesse, 'Send and bring him.

For we will not sit down till he comes here.' So he sent and brought him in. Now he was ruddy, with bright eyes, and good-looking. And the Lord said, 'Arise, anoint him; for this is the one!' Then Samuel took the horn of oil and anointed him in the midst of his brothers; and *the Spirit of the Lord* came upon David from that day forward. So Samuel arose and went to Ramah. But the Spirit of the Lord departed from Saul, and a distressing spirit from the Lord troubled him" (1 Samuel 16:11-14, emphasis mine).

The Holy Spirit is Here to Stay

The present time is the age of the Holy Spirit. Just as there will be no rebirth, death, or resurrection of Jesus Christ again, there will be no Pentecost again. Pentecost is done, once and for all. That day, the Holy Spirit took responsibility to lead the world.

But there *is* fresh infilling of the Spirit. Whenever God's people do God's work, the Holy Spirit comes afresh and empowers His servants to accomplish the task at hand. The Holy Spirit is in charge of the physical and spiritual activities of all creation. He fills His servants to do whatever is needed at that time and place. This sounds like a paradox, but it is what the Scriptures testify.

Peter, for example, was full of the Holy Spirit when he answered the Pharisees in Acts 4:8. But Peter was also full of the Holy Spirit in Acts 2 and when he pronounced God's judgment on Ananias and Sapphira in Acts 5:1-10. The apostles were full of the Holy Spirit when they prayed in Acts 4:31. Stephen was full of the Spirit when he preached in Acts 7:8-10 and Acts 8:54-60. Paul was full of the Holy Spirit when he rebuked Bar-Jesus, a false prophet, in Acts 13:4-12.

We need to be filled by the Holy Spirit every day. In all of these circumstances after Acts 2, when the apostles needed power, the Holy Spirit came upon them and empowered them to do God's work. Just as the preacher needs to be filled by the Spirit when he preaches, we need power from the Spirit to do God's work in our everyday lives. But this does not mean Pentecost is coming again. The time after Pentecost is the realm of the Holy Spirit, who works freely as the third person of the Trinity.

Every Christian is baptized by the Holy Spirit at his or her baptism. In baptism we receive the package of the gifts of the Holy Spirit. There is no Christian who does not possess the Holy Spirit (Romans 8:9), who is the seal for our salvation (Ephesians 1:13). "For He whom God has sent speaks the words of God, for God does not give the Spirit by measure" (John 3:34). But no one person has all the gifts of the Holy Spirit (1 Corinthians 12:1-11). Rather, all the gifts of grace are given to the church, and the Holy Spirit gives these gifts to individual people as He sees fit.

Now that we have seen the person and attributes of the Holy Spirit, we will look at His work in creation and the church.

Chapter Five

THE WORKS OF THE HOLY SPIRIT

The Holy Spirit is Creator. God sends out His Spirit in His work of creation, as the psalmist writes in Psalm 104:30, "You send forth Your Spirit, they are created; And You renew the face of the earth." It was the Holy Spirit who incubated the chaos of Genesis 1 before the earth took its present form, as it is written in Genesis 1:2: "The earth was without form, and void; and darkness was on the face of the deep. And the Spirit of God was hovering over the face of the waters."

In the midst of the earth being void and formless and under darkness and in the depth of the deep, the only hope was the Holy Spirit. Creation emerged by the command of God, step by step, over the span of six consecutive days from under the wings of the Holy Spirit to take its present form. Job poetically testifies that the heavens were adorned by the Spirit of God: "By His Spirit He adorned the heavens; His hand pierced the fleeing serpent" (Job 26:13).

This verse shows not only the works of the Holy Spirit in creation. It also teaches that creation was spiritual war between God and the fleeing serpent. It is common knowledge among theologians that the waters from under which creation emerged were a symbol of evil and chaos. The young man Elihu writes in Job 33:4 that the Spirit of God formed him and the breath of the Almighty gives him life, a concept reminiscent of Genesis 2:7, where it is written, "And the Lord God formed man of the dust of the ground, and breathed into his nostrils the breath of life; and man became a living being." Psalm 33:6 reflects this idea too: "By the word of the Lord the heavens were made, And all the host of them by the breath of His mouth."

The Holy Spirit Guides Us to All Truth

John writes, "However, when He, the Spirit of truth, has come, He will guide you into all truth; for He will not speak on His own authority, but whatever He hears He will speak; and He will tell you things to come" (John 16:13). The Holy Spirit doesn't only guide us to all truth. He *is* the Spirit of truth, in contrast to the devil, the father of lies in whom there is no truth (John 8:44). While the devil speaks from his own resources when he lies, the Holy Spirit does not speak on His own authority but instead hears from the Son (John 16:15) and declares His truth to us.

The other work of the Holy Spirit is glorifying Jesus in our hearts, our lives, and our worship. That is why Paul writes, "No one can say that Jesus is Lord except by the Holy Spirit" (1 Corinthians 12:3). Paul is clearly saying it is impossible to worship Jesus without the power of the Holy Spirit.

The Holy Spirit is Our Helper

John writes, "And I will pray the Father, and He will give you another Helper, that He may abide with you forever—the Spirit of truth, whom the world cannot receive, because it neither sees Him nor knows Him; but you know Him, for He dwells with you and will be in you" (John 14:16-17).

The Helper, or Paraclete in Greek, is our defender, counselor, advocate, and guide. Jesus was our Helper during His physical presence on the earth, and now that He has ascended to heaven, another Helper, the Holy Spirit, has come to replace Him. This is why Jesus said in John 16:7, "If I do not go away, the Helper will not come to you; but if I depart, I will send Him to you."

Jesus defended His disciples when the Pharisees accused them of transgressing the tradition of the elders (Matthew 15:1). He interceded for Peter: "Simon, Simon! Indeed, Satan has asked for you, that he may sift you as wheat. But I have prayed for you, that your faith should not fail; and when you have returned to Me, strengthen your brethren" (Luke 22:31-32). That is the role the Holy Spirit took when Jesus left the disciples in His care. Paul writes: "Likewise the Spirit also helps in our weaknesses. For we do not know what we should pray for as we ought, but the Spirit Himself makes intercession for us with groanings which cannot be uttered. Now He who searches the hearts knows what the mind of the Spirit is, because He makes intercession for the saints according to the will of God" (Romans 8:26-27). That is why it can be said that Jesus sent His disciples the Holy Spirit, who lived in their hearts and did exactly what Jesus did for them when He led them in person on the earth.

First Samuel 19:17-24 tells how the Holy Spirit guarded David: "Then Saul said to Michal, 'Why have you deceived me like this, and sent my enemy away, so that he has escaped?' And Michal answered Saul, 'He said to me, 'Let me go! Why should I kill you?' So David fled and escaped, and went to Samuel at Ramah, and told him all that Saul had done to him. And he and Samuel went and stayed in Naioth. Now it was told Saul, saying, 'Take note, David is at Naioth in Ramah!' Then Saul sent messengers to take David. And when they saw the group of prophets prophesying, and Samuel standing as leader over them, the Spirit of God came upon the messengers of Saul, and they also prophesied. And when Saul was told, he sent other messengers, and they prophesied likewise. Then Saul sent messengers again the third time, and they prophesied also. Then he also went to Ramah, and came to the great well that is at Sechu. So he asked, and said, 'Where are Samuel and David?' And someone said, 'Indeed they are at Naioth in Ramah.' So he went there to Naioth in Ramah. Then the Spirit of God was upon him also, and he went on and prophesied until he came to Naioth in Ramah. And he also stripped off his clothes and prophesied before Samuel in like manner, and lay down naked all that day and all that night. Therefore they say, 'Is Saul also among the prophets?'"

The Holy Spirit Empowers Us to Preach the Gospel.

The Holy Spirit empowered the disciples to testify about the gospel in unfavorable situations: "But you shall receive power when the Holy Spirit has come upon you; and you shall be witnesses to Me in Jerusalem, and in all Judea and Samaria, and to the end of the earth" (Acts 1:8). When the Holy Spirit arrived on the day of Pentecost, Peter, who was normally fearful, was full of confidence as he testified in front of some of the Jews who had participated in handing over Jesus to the gentiles (Acts 2:14; Acts 22-24), emphatically stating that "this Jesus God has raised up, of which we are all witnesses" (Acts 2:32). He also fearlessly asserted to the Jews gathered at the scene, "Therefore let all the house of Israel know assuredly that God has made this Jesus, whom you crucified, both Lord and Christ" (Acts 2:36), a concept unthinkable for the Jews to accept had the Holy Spirit not convinced them. The extraordinary power by which Peter preached captivated their attention, along with the testimony they heard preached in their mother tongues (the languages of different people from the Diaspora) by Galileans, who would have had no way to speak in their languages if it were not for the Holy Spirit.

Further testimonies of Peter in his sermons in Jerusalem coupled with the testimony of Stephen (Acts 7) challenged many Jews, including Saul of Tarsus, and converted them to faith in Jesus Christ. Peter boldly preaches, "The God of Abraham, Isaac, and Jacob, the God of our fathers, glorified His Servant Jesus, whom you delivered up and denied in the presence of Pilate" (Acts 3:13), and admonishes his listeners to "repent therefore and be converted, that your sins may be blotted out, so that times of refreshing may come from the presence of the Lord" (Acts 3:19). In his letter to the Thessalonians, Paul writes, "For our gospel did not come to you in word only, but also in power, and in the Holy Spirit and in much assurance, as you know what kind of men we were among you for your sake" (1 Thessalonians 1:5). It was the Holy Spirit who convicted the hearts of both Jews and gentiles and captivated them for Christ through the words of the apostles and extraordinary miracles. The apostle Peter testifies in his letter about the Old Testament prophets that "it was revealed that, not to themselves, but to us they were ministering the things which now have been reported to you through those who have preached the gospel to you by the Holy Spirit sent from heaven—things which angels desire to look into" (1 Peter 1:12). These and other Scriptures reveal the gospel was—and is—being preached by the power of the Holy Spirit from the beginning through today.

Every Christian Has the Holy Spirit.

According to the Scriptures, someone is a Christian because he or she is indwelt by the Holy Spirit. It is impossible to be a Christian without being baptized by the Holy Spirit. As Peter preached on the day of Pentecost: "Repent, and let every one of you be baptized in the name of Jesus Christ for the remission of sins; and you shall receive the gift of the Holy Spirit. For the promise is to you and to your children, and to all who are afar off, as many as the Lord our God will call" (Acts 2:38-39). Being baptized by the Holy Spirit is the very essence of being a Christian. Those who repent of their sins and are baptized receive the Holy Spirit and as a result become Christians.

Paul, too, contends the presence of the Holy Spirit in us is what makes us Christians. "So then, those who are in the flesh cannot please

God. But you are not in the flesh but in the Spirit, if indeed the Spirit of God dwells in you. Now if anyone does not have the Spirit of Christ, he is not His. And if Christ is in you, the body is dead because of sin, but the Spirit is life because of righteousness" (Romans 8:8-10).

In his epistle to the Ephesians, Paul uses two essential words: "sealed" and "guarantee." A seal is a mark of ownership. In the culture I come from, some wealthy individuals used to seal their cattle with a specific sign showing the animal belonged to that person. That made it easy to find any animal stolen from that owner. In the same manner, God has sealed all Christians with the Holy Spirit. The presence of the Holy Spirit in our lives is proof we are God's children. Paul says, "In Him you also trusted, after you heard the word of truth, the gospel of your salvation; in whom also, having believed, you were sealed with the Holy Spirit of promise, who is the guarantee of our inheritance until the redemption of the purchased possession, to the praise of His glory" (Ephesians 1:13-14).

God seals, or baptizes, His children with the Holy Spirit just one time at the time of Holy Baptism. In fact, the phrase "water baptism" doesn't exist at all in the Bible. John the Baptizer said, "I baptize you in water," but that isn't the baptism Jesus commanded His disciples to conduct (Matthew 28:19; Mark 16:15-16). Baptism after Jesus ascended and sent the Holy Spirit cannot be referred to as water baptism.

Paul also argues the presence of the Holy Spirit in our lives guarantees our inheritance in heaven until the day our redemption is publicly declared in front of the whole world. In other words, the Holy Spirit is the down payment, or the earnest of our inheritance. He explains: "For all the promises of God in Him are Yes, and in Him Amen, to the glory of God through us. Now He who establishes us with you in Christ and has anointed us is God, who also has sealed us and given us the Spirit in our hearts as a guarantee" (2 Corinthians 1:20-22).

In addition, Paul commands us to be aware that the Holy Spirit lives in us through the words we speak, advising us that our conversations should edify people and not tear them apart. "Let no corrupt word proceed out of your mouth, but what is good for necessary edification, that it may impart grace to the hearers. And do not grieve the Holy Spirit of God, by whom you were sealed for the day of redemption. Let all bitterness, wrath, anger, clamor, and evil speaking be put away from you, with all malice. And be kind to one another, tenderhearted, forgiving one another, just as God in Christ forgave you" (Ephesians 4:29-32). He warns we must not only choose our words but also control our thoughts, as the Holy Spirit is a person resident in our hearts: he can be grieved by how we carry ourselves.

The filling of the Holy Spirit is not a one-time action. In Ephesians 5, it is explained as the continuous control of the Holy Spirit of our lives. Paul writes: "Therefore do not be unwise, but understand what the will of the Lord is. And do not be drunk with wine, in which is dissipation; but be filled with the Spirit, speaking to one another in psalms and hymns and spiritual songs, singing and making melody in your heart to the Lord, giving thanks always for all things to God the Father in the name of our Lord Jesus Christ, submitting to one another in the fear of God" (Ephesians 5:17-21).

As they selected deacons, the apostles searched for men like this—"men of good reputation, full of the Holy Spirit and wisdom, whom we may appoint over this business" (Acts 6:3). These were men that lived in the state of fullness of the Spirit as He continuously controlled their thoughts and words and actions.

Being Filled with the Holy Spirit Is a Means of Receiving Power for Immediate Ministry.

The Holy Spirit sometimes empowers us to do a certain immediate task. We see this in the life of Samson: "The Spirit of the Lord came mightily upon him, and he tore the lion apart as one would have torn apart a young goat, though he had nothing in his hand. But he did not tell his father or his mother what he had done" (Judges 14:6).

We also see this on the day of Pentecost, when the apostles "were all filled with the Holy Spirit and began to speak with other tongues, as the Spirit gave them utterance" (Acts 2:4). Later in Acts, when the apostles had prayed, "the place where they were assembled together was shaken; and they were all filled with the Holy Spirit, and they spoke the word of God with boldness" (Acts 4:31).

Acts 10:44-46 recounts that "while Peter was still speaking these words, the Holy Spirit fell upon all those who heard the word. And those of the circumcision who believed were astonished, as many as came with Peter, because the gift of the Holy Spirit had been poured out on the Gentiles also. For they heard them speak with tongues and magnify God."

Another instance of the Holy Spirit's immediate empowering occurs in Acts 13:9-11, when Paul speaks to a sorcerer: "Then Saul, who also is called Paul, filled with the Holy Spirit, looked intently at him and said, 'O full of all deceit and all fraud, you son of the devil, you enemy of all righteousness, will you not cease perverting the straight ways of the Lord? And now, indeed, the hand of the Lord is upon you, and you shall be blind, not seeing the sun for a time.' And immediately a dark mist fell on him, and he went around seeking someone to lead him by the hand."

These portions of the Bible make it clear that we need to do God's work, including preaching as Peter did in Acts 2 and as the other apostles did when they performed healings and other miracles. The Holy Spirit does not come to us without his gifts. We will discuss these gifts in the following chapter.

Chapter 6

THE GIFTS OF GRACE

> "Now concerning spiritual gifts, brethren, I do not want you to be ignorant: You know that you were Gentiles, carried away to these dumb idols, however you were led. Therefore I make known to you that no one speaking by the Spirit of God calls Jesus accursed, and no one can say that Jesus is Lord except by the Holy Spirit. There are diversities of gifts, but the same Spirit. There are differences of ministries, but the same Lord. And there are diversities of activities, but it is the same God who works all in all. But the manifestation of the Spirit is given to each one for the profit of all."
> 1 Corinthians 12:1-7

The very planting of the church was done through the gifts of preaching, teaching, healing, and exorcism. As a result, the gifts of grace started to manifest in the lives of believers. It is natural to assume that questions about these gifts popped up among believers. Paul takes the initiative to explain the spiritual things—*ton pnumatikon* (των πνευματικων)—being manifested among the believers in Corinth, and we know 1 Corinthians was written in response to some of the questions the Corinthians had at the time, but I don't see any indication the issue of spiritual things was on the list of their questions. Yet, the lack of obvious enquiries about gifts of grace among the list of questions sent by the Corinthian Christians to Paul does not prove the absence of discussion regarding the discord in the use of the gifts of grace in the Corinthian worship service.

As he begins his discourse on the gifts of grace, Paul reminds his readers they were idol worshipers before they came to Christ and explains that it is the Holy Spirit who enables them to confess that Jesus is Lord (1 Corinthians 12:1-3). Paul makes it clear these are different kinds of gifts by using the word that is translated as "gifts of grace": *charismaton* (ξαρισματων). We know *karis* (ξαρισ) is "grace" in Greek. Grace is a free gift God gives without us making any effort. The gifts of grace Paul writes about are actually the manifestations of the Holy Spirit Himself. The Holy Spirit manifests Himself in His church through these things of the Spirit (τον πνυευματικων), or the gifts of grace.

The Greek used to denote "gifts of grace" in 1 Corinthians 12:7 is "manifestation of the Spirit," *Phanerosis ta pneumatos* (Φανερωσισ τα Πνεματου), when transliterated. Phanerosis (Φανερωσισ) is "exhibition, expression, bestowment, or manifestation."[58] It comes from the verb *phanero* (φανερω), which means "to render apparent or manifestly declare."[59] Paul uses the same word (φανερωσισ) in 2 Corinthians 4:2, where he writes, "But we have renounced the hidden things of shame, not walking in craftiness nor handling the word of God deceitfully, but by manifestation of the truth commending ourselves to every man's conscience in the sight of God."

The Greek is *phanerosis ten aletheia* (φανερωσει τησ αλεθειασ), or "manifestation of the truth." The derivative of the same word is used in Colossians 1:26, which talks about "the mystery which has been hidden from ages and from generations, but now has been revealed to His saints." *The New Revised Standard Version* translates the phrase as "reveled to his saints," while the *New American Standard Bible 1995* translates Colossians 1:26 as "was manifested to His saints."

There are other instances in the Bible in which the derivatives of fanerw are used, including Romans 1:19, which addresses the manifestation of the truth about God; Romans 16:26, where Paul speaks of the manifestation of the mystery of the good news that had been kept secret; and Colossians 4:4; 1 Peter 1:20; and John 14:21-22. Just as He manifests His truth in Colossians 1:26 and Romans 1:19, God manifests His Spirit through the gifts of grace. We know there isn't any church where the gifts of grace are not working for all spiritual activities, including preaching, teaching, counseling, and singing.

The Purpose of the Gifts of Grace

Gifts of grace are given for the edification and service of the body of Christ, the church. It is written: "But he who prophesies speaks edification and exhortation and comfort to men. He who speaks in a tongue edifies himself, but he who prophesies edifies the church" (1 Corinthians 14:3-4). It is also written, "Even so you, since you are zealous for spiritual gifts, let it be for the edification of the church that you seek to excel " (1 Corinthians 14:12). The gifts of grace are not the possession of the person to whom they are given. We make a mistake when we say someone "has the gift of." Nobody personally has a gift. Nobody owns a gift. The gifts belong to God and the church. We are only stewards of these gifts for the edification of the church. The proper saying should be, "The church has________________gift of grace in the service of ____________."

The gifts of grace are given for the common good of both believers and nonbelievers, as it is written in 1 Corinthians 12:7: "But the manifestation of the Spirit is given to each one for the profit of all." In 1 Corinthians 14:26, we read: "How is it then, brethren? Whenever you come together, each of you has a psalm, has a teaching, has a tongue, has a revelation, has an interpretation. Let all things be done for edification." The gifts are not designed for personal benefit. Anyone with gifts should be part of a local church gathering, or *ekklesia* (εκκλησια). Even though He calls us individually, God doesn't know us outside of the local church. We must be part of the local church. That is the reason Jesus said to pray "Our" Father and not "my" Father in the Lord's Prayer. But that does not mean God doesn't care about us as individual Christians." It means that every Christian should be part of the local church.

The amazing thing is that God wants to manifest His Spirit among us, even though we are fallen and imperfect men and women. Paul writes to the Corinthian church: "I thank my God always concerning you for the grace of God which was given to you by Christ Jesus, that you were enriched in everything by Him in all utterance and all knowledge, even as the testimony of Christ was confirmed in you, so that you come short in no gift, eagerly waiting for the revelation of our Lord Jesus Christ" (1 Corinthians 1:4-7). There is a tendency, as Paul notes, to be haughty or feel superior when the gifts of grace manifest themselves in our ministry. As the Spirit functions in our ministry, we can get caught up and carried away in our thinking that we have something to do with it instead of giving all glory to God. We need to be careful as we minister with His gifts, for God does not bestow them on us because we impress Him by our obedience. The gifts of grace are not given because we are holy. The gifts are not given because we are better Christians. Rather, God gives gifts because of His grace in accordance with the measure of faith He has given us. In Romans 12:3 Paul writes, "For I say, through the grace given to me, to everyone who is among you, not to think of himself more highly than he ought to think, but to think soberly, as God has dealt to each one a measure of faith."

In another portion of 1 Corinthians, Paul writes to Corinthians who are arrogant because they have been given gifts of grace manifested in speaking. "Now these things, brethren, I have figuratively transferred to myself and Apollos for your sakes, that you may learn in us not to think beyond what is written, that none of you may be puffed up on behalf of one against the other. For who makes you differ from another? And what do you have that you did not receive? Now if you did indeed receive it, why do you boast as if you had not received it?" (1 Corinthians 4:6-7). In Romans 12:6 he writes, "Having then gifts differing according to the grace that is given to us, let us use them: if prophecy, let us prophesy in proportion to our faith."

We need to fight off haughtiness and other unproductive behaviors as the gifts function in our lives. We should always remember we cannot impress God. Gifts are *charismata*—gifts of grace. It is grace that enables us to serve as we do. Grace is the free gift we were given as the result of the work accomplished on the cross through the Lord Jesus Christ. Grace was not attained for free—Jesus worked for it—but to us it is given for free.

Spiritual Gifts and Christian Maturity

The same Holy Spirit who gives us natural talents also gives us our spiritual gifts. (Natural talents and spiritual gifts are not contradictory, for they are given by the same Holy Spirit.) It is not by the fervency of our prayers that we impress God and receive gifts of grace. Yet the church is ordered to pray for the gifts of grace (1 Corinthians 14:1). We should pray for the actualization of the gifts in our lives, for God has already given these gifts to the church through individual members at the time of holy baptism. These gifts are given for the growth and edification of the body of Christ (1 Corinthians 14:26) and belong to God and the church.

Speaking in tongues or having another gift of the Holy Spirit does not make us godly; godliness and gifts of the Holy Spirit are two separate things. Godliness is character that results from obedience to the word of God and the Holy Spirit. Likewise, there is a difference between serving by the gifts of grace and being a spiritually mature person. Spirituality does not express itself in speaking in tongues or prophecy. Rather, spirituality expresses itself in daily life. People can witness it. It is tangible. A mature person is controlled by—and is full of—the Holy Spirit (1 Thessalonians 5:18).

Many gifts of grace were in action at the time Paul wrote his epistle to the Corinthian church. Its members were enriched with all speech and all knowledge (1 Corinthians 1:6), but Paul criticizes the church as carnal (1 Corinthians 3:1-4). The Corinthian church was not spiritual even though its people had been given the gifts of grace.

> "And I, brethren, could not speak to you as to spiritual people but as to carnal, as to babes in Christ" (1 Corinthians 3:1). Some church members were adulterers (1 Corinthians 5:1-2); others went to the civil court to settle disagreements among themselves (1 Corinthians 6:1-8). They had many spiritual gifts, but these gifts did not transform them into spiritual people. They were still carnal. The church had the challenge of being served by spiritual babes to whom God had given the ministry of serving in gifts of grace. Paul, therefore, urged church members to grow to maturity: "Watch, stand fast in the faith, be brave, be strong" (1 Corinthians 16:13).

There is no excuse to continue in immaturity. Every Christian is expected to mature in love and self-control. The most important thing in Christian life is to evaluate our motives in whatever we do, whether in service or in ministry. The Holy Spirit is given for those who obey God (Acts 5:32), but He is given to the whole church. Obedience in this context is not being perfect in keeping the Law of Moses. It is obedience to faith or believing in Jesus Christ.

Chapter 7

BIBLICAL COMMANDS ABOUT THE GIFTS OF GRACE

From the beginning, the Lord has always instructed His servants how His work should be done. God, who could have made the whole creation in a fraction of a second, created the world in six days, explaining the process involved. While He could have wiped away Egypt and removed His people from there in a second, He used ten miracles, after which Pharaoh finally submitted. He ordered Moses to make the Ark of the Covenant from a certain tree and gave him the width, the length, and the height of the Ark. He instructed Moses to put the tablets in the Ark and told him how to make the tabernacle, the arrangement of the Cherubim, the Holy of Holies, the place of bath, and the altar of sacrifice. He advised who should carry the Ark of the Covenant and how it should be carried. He told Joshua how the Ark of the Covenant should cross the Jordan River and who from among the children of Israel should put their feet in the Jordan first. This is how God wanted things to be done among His people. Those who didn't obey His instructions paid the price.

The Bible's instructions about speaking in tongues and using the other gifts of grace should not be seen differently from other instructions Paul gives in different parts of his epistles and even those given to God's people in the Old Testament. All gifts are for the benefit of the church and for the glory of God, and their recipients should follow the instructions given in the Bible for their use. Gifts used without biblical knowledge can be detrimental to our faith.

1 Thessalonians 5:19: Do not quench the Spirit (Το πνευμα μη σβεννυτε)

The meaning of the Greek *sbenute* (σβεννυτε) from the verb *sbenumai* (σβεννυμι) is "extinguish, put out, or quench."[60] To quench the Spirit means to resist His influence, like trying to smother a fire. Therefore, this verse assumes the Spirit is a fire that is already burning. The other assumption is that the Spirit can be extinguished or smothered where He is burning—that humans can put out the burning fire of the Holy Spirit in their lives.

This shows how humble the Holy Spirit is. He does not force Himself on us. Just like Jesus in Revelation 3:20, the Holy Spirit waits, knocking on the doors of our hearts to work in our lives. This does not mean humans can stop God from working. (If humans could stop God's work, they would have stopped Jesus from performing miracles in the Jewish synagogues.) Rather, this means people can stop the working of God in their own lives and ministries. Paul advises that if the Spirit is burning in your life and ministry, do not extinguish Him. Do not put out or restrain the Spirit's fire. One of the fundamental rules of walking with God is that we should not say no to the influence of the Spirit of God. That is an error the church should stay away from.

1 Thessalonians 5:20: Do not despise prophecies (Prophetias me exoustheneite) *(Προφητειασ μη εξουσθενειτε)*

The Greek word *exoutheneite* (εξουθενειτε) comes from the verb *exoutheneo* (εξουθενεω), which means "to despise, treat with contempt, look down on, count as nothing, or reject."[61] *Strong's Exhaustive Concordance of the Bible* translates exoutheneo (εξουθενεω) to mean "contemptible, despise, least esteemed, or set at naught or nothing."[62] The assumption here is that prophecy can be looked down upon. This is a temptation for all of us, as we have heard many false prophecies that didn't come true.

Paul gives instructions to the church not to believe everything spoken as a prophecy. He advises the church to test all things, and in this context, test prophecy. We should not be afraid to test prophecy, because we are in God's house, not in some notorious deity's worship system where we are stricken for testing statements uttered by spirits. We have the commandment and the authority to test prophecies.

In the Bible, those who test prophecies are appreciated for doing so. The angel or pastor of the church of Ephesus is commended for being discerning: "And you have tested those who say they are apostles and are not, and have found them liars" (Revelation 2:2). Those who don't test claims are criticized. In Revelation 2:14 the church at Pergamos is reprimanded: "You have there those who hold the doctrine of Balaam, who taught Balak to put a stumbling block before the children of Israel, to eat things sacrificed to idols, and to commit sexual immorality." The church of Thyatira is also criticized: "Nevertheless I have a few things against you, because you allow that woman Jezebel, who calls herself a prophetess, to teach and seduce My servants to commit sexual immorality and eat things sacrificed to idols" (Revelation 2:20).

Discerning spirits and unraveling false apostles and prophets is not contempt for the Spirit in any way or sense. It is a necessary work to decipher between the true and the false. It is a work done to differentiate between evil and good. This helps the church abstain from evil and work with the good. In doing this, we serve God and His church.

I have faced people who threaten that anyone who second guesses them will be smitten by God. The congregation may wait in fear that their pastor will be punished by God, as those who are tricked expect to be smitten. But if we discern messages, sermons, and prophecies in the fear of the Lord, we will not encounter evil. Instead, we will uncover lies and show the church those threats are empty. We will expose those who think God will do everything they utter and those who are carried away in the heat of the worship service.

1 Corinthians 14:28: Do not speak in tongues in public without interpretation

"Whenever you come together, each of you has a psalm, has a teaching, has a tongue, has a revelation, has an interpretation. Let all things be done for edification. If anyone speaks in a tongue, let there be two or at the most three, each in turn, and let one interpret. But if there is no interpreter, let him keep silent in church, and let him speak to himself and to God" (1 Corinthians 14:26-28). This means a Christian worship service has psalms, teaching, tongues, revelations, and interpretations of tongues ministered by different people in the congregation according to their gifts.

While all other ministries need no further discussion in this passage, the gift of speaking in tongues is accompanied by a command that tongues should be interpreted into intelligible language. Paul teaches that people should not speak loudly in tongues in public worship if there is no interpretation into a language others can understand. People can speak in tongues in church to themselves and to God silently in public worship. But they shouldn't raise their voices as if they have a message. The reason is to have order in church so a message can be communicated. Paul even warns that uncontrolled tongue utterances are not good for the reputation of the church in the community in which it functions. Here is his warning: "Therefore if the whole church comes together in one place, and all speak with tongues, and there come in those who are uninformed or unbelievers, will they not say that you are out of your mind?" (1 Corinthians 14:23)

Those who speak in tongues should know how to control themselves. If tongues are not interpreted, outsiders or unbelieving visitors might be confused or consider the people speaking in tongues out of their minds. If not interpreted, tongues can be counterproductive and portray the church to unbelieving visitors as a place of out-of-mind babblers.

1 Corinthians 14:39: Do not forbid speaking in tongues in public worship

> "Therefore, brethren, desire earnestly to prophesy, and do not forbid to speak with tongues" (1 Corinthians 14:39).

All communication should be meaningful. It should be intelligible. But in the quest for intelligibility we should not exclude unintelligibility as long as it is interpreted into intelligible language or into language the people in worship understand.

It is possible that in Corinth there were efforts to ban tongues altogether and that Paul may have been responding to these efforts. Speaking in tongues should not be banned from Christian worship. Paul does not forbid speaking in tongues; rather, his command is that all tongues should be interpreted into a language understandable to worshipers.

When tongues are interpreted, they can be used to serve God and His people. They reveal the secrets of the hearts of people and edify everyone, for the messages are intelligible. Speaking in tongues generates power and gives joy and strength in Christian life. We should not stop people from practicing their gifts or sit idly in the church without the desire to serve the Lord with the gifts of the Spirit. The gift of tongues is beneficial to the speaker in private prayers and to the congregation in public worship when it is interpreted.

In former days in the Ethiopian Evangelical Church Mekane Yesus, people were persecuted just for practicing gifts of grace like prophecy and tongues. Now we are in a time where there is no order in worship because people have no respect for order in a worship service. We should press for order according to the Scriptures, but our discomfort with the disobedience of immature Christians and the bold refusal of those who think we are against God and the working of the Holy Spirit should not lead us to forbid speaking in tongues as long as they are interpreted.

1 Corinthians 14:26-27: Multiple people should not speak in tongues in public worship simultaneously

Multiple people can speak in tongues in a worship service one after another. What Paul teaches is that multiple people should not speak in tongues simultaneously in a worship service.

The key is that everything uttered in a worship service should be intelligible and edifying to the congregation. The church is the place of order. One can see all of God's creation and understand that God is the God of order. Public worship is for all to understand. Therefore, elements of the worship service should be orderly and respectful. A message shouldn't feed the emotion of an individual in the congregation while the rest of the congregation wonders what he or she is saying. That kind of utterance is a waste of time, for it is not presented in the language the people understand and therefore does not edify the hearers. In some charismatic circles spirituality is measured by whether someone speaks in tongues. It is common to encounter pastors and preachers speaking in tongues in the midst of their sermons without any interpretation just to let the congregation know they are the ones who speak in tongues or that they are spiritual.

Another common unbiblical assumption is that the working of

the Holy Spirit is measured by multiple worshipers loudly speaking in tongues in the worship service simultaneously. In Acts 2, where all present spoke in tongues, the people who had come to celebrate Pentecost heard and understood the message of the apostles in their own languages. There were 120 people (Acts 1:15) in that meeting who were speaking in tongues. If all of those people had spoken at once, how could others have heard the message in their own languages and been converted? There couldn't have been order if all 120 people had spoken simultaneously. If that had been the case, no one would have understood his mother tongue from among the 120 people loudly speaking at the same time. Therefore, it is rational to believe they took turns speaking of the great works of God. That must have taken some time to do, but that is the only logical conclusion to explain how all of those Diaspora people could have understood the message the Holy Spirit was conveying on that Pentecost Day.

1 Corinthians 12:26-31: All tongues are interpretable

The gift of speaking in tongues is called glossolalia (γλοσσαλα–λια). Some argue that tongues meant for interpretation are different from tongues generally spoken. But there is no indication of this in the Scriptures in the Greek text. All throughout the epistles of Paul where this gift is explained, the derivatives of the same Greek word are used. Look at 1 Corinthians 12:10: *Tero gene glosson, allo de eremeneia glosson* (τερω γενη γλωσσων, αλλω δε ερμηνεια γλωσσων), which means "to another kind of tongues" and "to another interpretation of tongues." The words for "tongues" in the Greek are all derivatives of γλοσσα.

"If anyone speaks in a tongue, let there be two or at the most three, each in turn, and let one interpret. But if there is no interpreter, let him keep silent in church, and let him speak to himself and to God"

(1 Corinthians 14:27-28). The Greek translation is:

> "ειτε γλωσσαη τισ λαλει, κατα δυο η το πλειστον τρεισ κασ ανα μεροσ, και εισ δειρμηεϖευετω. εαν δε μη η διερμη-νευτησ. σεγατω εν εκκλησια, εατω δε λαλειτο και το θεω."

All tongues are interpretable—and, in fact, all tongues are given to the church specifically to be interpreted when spoken in public. It is up to the speakers to discern whether God has given them a message that can be spoken in tongues and then interpreted. If they are not sure whether God intends to give a message to the congregation through tongues and interpretation, they should speak to themselves and God in silence, even in public worship. Who is going to benefit when tongues are spoken publicly without interpretation? It is obvious God and His people do not benefit. If we are prompted to speak in tongues in public, we must also pray for the gift of interpretation.

The idea that some tongues are interpretable, and others are not, comes from the 1962 Amharic translation of the Bible, which is what most Ethiopians who understand Amharic read. The Pentecostal preachers used this to fit their understanding about interpretable and uninterpretable tongues. Because of this translation error, many reject the original intention for which the gift of speaking in tongues was given to the church: to bring a message in a language the people understand. As a result, some classify the gift of speaking in tongues into two categories: tongues that are meant to be interpreted in corporate worship service, and tongues that cannot be interpreted and are rather a gift for private prayer or are spoken in public at the prompting of the Spirit without interpretation. But this notion doesn't exist in the teachings of Paul and has created conflict within churches. Many pastors, in fact, have been mislabeled as opponents of the works of the Holy Spirit just because they want to bring to their churches the right intention of the Holy Spirit when He gave the church the gift of tongues.

1 Corinthians 12:30: Not all speak in tongues (Μη παντεσ γλωσσαισ λαλουσιν)

The notion that everyone should speak in tongues is completely foreign in the Bible. The assumption that people who don't speak in tongues have problems in their lives has created two kinds of Christians: those who speak in tongues and those who don't.

All gifts are not given to all people. God gives gifts selectively to different people according to His own desire. The gift of tongues is not a universal gift given to everyone. Gifts are given according to the will of the Spirit and not according to the desire of a certain Christian (1 Corinthians 12:4-11). 1 Corinthians 12:27-30 makes it clear all gifts are not given to one person. Speaking in tongues is just one of the gifts God gives to edify the church and individual Christians.

People should not blame themselves—and others should not blame them—for not speaking in tongues. People without the gift of speaking in tongues should not think they lack something. Much damage is done to people when speaking in tongues is seen as a gift every Christian must have. I want to emphatically assure you there is nothing wrong with those who have not received the gift of tongues. We are all sinners, and there are many things wrong with us. But the lack of the gift of speaking in tongues is not a sign of having a problem; it just means it is not in God's plan for a particular person to have this particular gift. God has given that person a different gift to use in a better way. They have another gift of grace.

People also should not misuse the gift of tongues as if it is given to brag how favored they are by God. I am among those who have received the gift of tongues. I pray with tongues in private and in worship services, quietly speaking to myself and to God. If we who have been given this gift sense we are trying to show off, we must stop and repent.

1 Corinthians 14:29-31: There should not be multiple prophecies simultaneously in public worship

One of the gifts that builds the congregation is prophesy, and we should desire to prophecy earnestly through teaching, preaching, and direct prediction. "Let two or three prophets speak, and let the others judge. But if anything is revealed to another who sits by, let the first keep silent. For you can all prophesy one by one, that all may learn and all may be encouraged. And the spirits of the prophets are subject to the prophets. For God is not the author of confusion but of peace, as in all the churches of the saints" (1 Corinthians 14:29-33).

In these verses Paul lays out the appropriate and orderly way for prophecy in Christian worship. His exhortation assumes there were more than three prophets at a time in the Corinthian worship service. But Paul recommends two or at most three prophets take turns bringing messages from God to the congregation. He even expects great restraint when something important is revealed while another person is speaking, saying the first person should stop speaking and let the newly revealed message be spoken. This takes the highest command of one's ego—to let another person bring a fresh message. The assumption here is that the latter message is the most up-to-date thought of God; the new message does not negate the former message but instead includes it. The gift of prophecy is not functioning as Paul instructs, and we must pray that gifts of grace, including prophecy, may function in our public worship.

1 Corinthians 14:29 Every utterance is up for judgment and discernment

In the early church, where the gifts of grace were revealed to infant local churches as entirely new experiences, every utterance was to be judged or discerned simultaneously as it was being delivered. Paul's command in 1 Corinthians 14:29 to "let two or three speak, and let the others judge" assumes two groups: a group of the utterers of prophecy, tongues, and interpretations and a group of discerners. While those who bring messages utter what God wants to speak to the people, discerners determine whether the messages are from God, the flesh, or demons. Discerners do a great service to the congregation, providing spiritual control in order to avoid the confusion and harm that come from demons and from the utterers' personal assumptions about what they think is the message of God.

The present situation in churches in Ethiopia and the South in general is not the same as in biblical times. Those who utter prophecy or tongues consider themselves perfect and are offended if someone tries to correct them. Other worshipers also consider these people perfect. In some places it is considered an offense to correct them. Those who try to save the congregations from harm and confusion are considered to be against the work of God. Some who prophesy in charismatic worship both in Ethiopia and in the United States among diaspora Oromo, Tigrean, Eritrean, and Ethiopian churches even threaten the wrath of God on those who correct them for the good of the ministry. These people frighten the common Christian to the point that some don't follow up on whether a certain prophetic utterance has taken place. If what is predicted about them does not take place, most blame themselves for lacking faith.

I have also encountered people who claim the power of tongues or prophecy is at times overwhelming to control. Paul teaches otherwise as he ascertains that "the spirits of the prophets are subject to the prophets." He adds that "God is not the author of confusion but of peace, as in all the churches of the saints" (Ου γαρ εστιν ακταστα–σιασ Ο Θεοσ αλλα ειρηνησ). We need no more arguments than these emphatic expressions by the most experienced speaker of tongues, Paul himself, who expresses in 1 Corinthians 14:18, "I thank my God I speak with tongues more than you all."

Chapter 8

THE GIFT OF TONGUES

The gift of tongues should be encouraged in Christian worship and private prayer. When God wants to bring a message in public worship through tongues, that message should be interpreted into a language people in attendance can understand.

What Does Being Filled by the Holy Spirit Mean?

Being filled with the Spirit means being under the guidance and control of the Holy Spirit. "And do not be drunk with wine, in which is dissipation; but be filled with the Spirit," Paul says in Ephesians 5:18. Here, Paul teaches the Ephesians not to lose control of their faculties or let alcohol control their thinking. He commands them to be controlled by the Holy Spirit. We need to be under the influence of the Holy Spirit all of the time.

The Bible teaches different meanings of being filled by the Holy Spirit. People are full of the Holy Spirit when they heal others. They are full of the Holy Spirit when they defeat enemies. Being filled by the Holy Spirit can also be about power coming on people to do specific things, like Samson killing the Philistines or Paul blinding Elymas.

In some congregations, those who speak in tongues are considered full of the Spirit, while those who don't speak in tongues are considered not full of the Holy Spirit. This incorrect interpretation was introduced when the Pentecostal movement started on Azusa Street in Los Angeles in 1900.[63] There is no place in the Bible that states speaking in tongues is the sign of being filled by the Holy Spirit. There are people who don't speak in tongues but who are still full of the Holy Spirit. There are people who don't speak in tongues but who still perform miracles, exorcise demons, and plant churches. The apostles speak in tongues in Acts 2, but this is not the same kind of tongues Paul teaches about in his epistles. Moreover, Paul teaches tongues are just gifts, not signs of being filled by the Spirit.

"Now you are the body of Christ, and members individually. And God has appointed these in the church: first apostles, second prophets, third teachers, after that miracles, then gifts of healings, helps, administrations, varieties of tongues. Are all apostles? Are all prophets? Are all teachers? Are all workers of miracles? Do all have gifts of healings? Do all speak with tongues? Do all interpret? But earnestly desire the best gifts. And yet I show you a more excellent way" (1 Corinthians 12:27-31).

The Greek requires a no for all the questions Paul asks: "μη παντεσ απὸστελοι?" (surely not all are apostles), μη παντεσ προφεται (surely not all are prophets), *Me pantes glossais lalousin* (μη παντεσ γλωσσαισ λαλουσιν) (surely not all speak in tongues)."

All are not apostles or prophets or miracle workers or teachers. By the same reasoning, Paul argues all do not speak in tongues. This is because speaking in tongues is a gift and not a sign of being filled by the Holy Spirit.

The Two Types of Tongues

Two types of tongues are mentioned in the New Testament. Xenolalia (speaking in a different but intelligible language) is mentioned in Acts 2:1-4. Glossolalia (speaking in unintelligible language) is mentioned in the Pauline Epistles (Romans 12:3-8; 1 Corinthians 12:1-11; 1 Corinthians 12:27-31; 1 Corinthians 14:1-39; Ephesians 4:7-16).

In Acts 10 the first group of gentiles received the Holy Spirit in the city of Caesarea. They spoke in tongues (glossolalia) (λαλυτον γλο–σαισ). It is not expressed whether this was glossolalia or xenolalia. In Acts 19:1-7 people received the Holy Spirit and spoke in tongues. But we do not get the impression that others heard them speaking in intelligible languages. The apostles spoke in intelligible tongues (xenolalia) on the day of Pentecost so other nationalities could understand their message. This reversed the curse of Babel, where God confused the language of humankind so the ensuing divisions would ultimately drive people to Him.[64]

While God mixed up the tongues of people in Genesis 11 to confuse them because of their attitude, God's intention is always to communicate clearly with His people. It was only when Israel disobeyed God that He spoke to them in foreign tongues through their enemies. Paul writes, "Therefore tongues are for a sign, not to those who believe but to unbelievers; but prophesying is not for unbelievers but for those who believe" (1 Corinthians 14:22). Paul quotes Isaiah 28:11-12, where God judged His people for not listening to Him and talked to them in the language of their enemies by deporting them from their own land. This is the second time God punished people using language.

But at the end of the day, God's intention is always to bring people back to Him. It is this sentiment that resonates in Paul's arguments about tongues (*glossolalia*) in 1 Corinthians 14. God uses languages unintelligible both to the speaker and the hearer to communicate His message to those who resist His calling. Paul writes: "Therefore if the whole church comes together in one place, and all speak with tongues, and there come in those who are uninformed or unbelievers, will they not say that you are out of your mind? But if all prophesy, and an unbeliever or an uninformed person comes in, he is convinced by all, he is convicted by all. And thus the secrets of his heart are revealed;

and so, falling down on his face, he will worship God and report that God is truly among you" (1 Corinthians 14:23-25).

The gift of interpretation of tongues reverses the curse on language as a means to separate people. It transforms the curse of unintelligibility into understanding and intelligibility. It breaks the sense of feeling alien to one another. While God broke the wall of differences by speaking directly to Diaspora Jews in their mother tongue in Jerusalem on the day of Pentecost, in glossolalia God breaks the wall of differences by the gift of interpretation of tongues.

Glossolalia (γλοσολαλια)

In 1 Corinthians 12:10, unintelligible language as a gift of grace (γλοσσολαλια, or glossolalia) is introduced into the discussion of language in the Bible for the first time. Glossolalia is utterance that should be accompanied by another gift called *ermeneia glossa* (ερ–μηνεια γλωσσων)—interpretation of tongues so both the speaker and the audience may understand. Glossolalia and interpretation of tongues are two separate gifts of the Spirit by their own rights.

The gift of glossolalia is given to the church for two purposes:

1. For edification in private prayer or in tight groups to which visitors are not invited.
2. To convey a message, when interpreted, for the edification of the congregation when used in public worship.

Only for these two purposes—and nothing more—is glossolalia intended as a gift of grace to the church of Christ.

Xenolalia

Xeno means "alien," "strange", or "guest"; it's used in the formation of compound words such as xenophobia, which means "hatred of the alien or stranger."[65] Xenolalia means "alien or strange tongue or language"; the languages the apostles spoke in Jerusalem on the day of Pentecost were xeno to the Jerusalem Jews, while they were mother tongues to the Diaspora Jews.

This is the type of speaking in tongues that took place in Acts 2. A Galilean Jew being led by the Holy Spirit could speak Coptic, Italian, Greek, Latin, or Spanish on the day of Pentecost. In the crowd were also proselytes, or gentiles who had converted to Judaism. They spoke the languages of the countries of the Diaspora Jews and the proselytes. Jews who had come from different geographic and ethnic localities could hear their own languages being spoken by these Galilean Jews. In this way the Holy Spirit preached to Diaspora Jews, who represented all of us since they came from various parts of the world and spoke different languages in addition to Hebrew. The Holy Spirit did this miracle to pave the way for the preaching of the gospel among Jews around the world and eventually to all the gentiles.

People speak of incidences of xenolalia in our days too. I have not encountered it myself, but I believe if God has a purpose in doing so He can make people speak in languages they do not know but that are native languages for others. The common practice, though, is for missionaries to go to people of a different culture and learn their language as they live among them. It is through that kind of immersion that missionaries can bring the gospel to many parts of the world, including my own people, the Oromo.

Language: The Result of Curse and Blessing

Language is a means of communication. God used language to create the world. Then God and the first family conversed in Genesis 1:28-30: "Then God blessed them, and God said to them, 'Be fruitful and multiply; fill the earth and subdue it; have dominion over the fish of the sea, over the birds of the air, and over every living thing that moves on the earth.' And God said, 'See, I have given you every herb that yields seed which is on the face of all the earth, and every tree whose fruit yields seed; to you it shall be for food. Also, to every beast of the earth, to every bird of the air, and to everything that creeps on the earth, in which there is life, I have given every green herb for food'; and it was so."

We don't know what language God used to create the world or what language God and humanity used in the garden of Eden. Yet by Genesis 3 the communication between God and humanity was already strained. The woman had a conversation with the serpent that led to the duo eating the forbidden fruit. Afterward, the husband and the wife didn't want to talk to God and hid from His face. Later they blamed one another when God talked to them in the garden.

The woman was met with a clear choice. She could believe God, who said, "Of every tree of the garden you may freely eat; but of the tree of the knowledge of good and evil you shall not eat, for in the day that you eat of it you shall surely die" (Genesis 2:16-17). Or she could believe the serpent, who said, "You will not surely die. For God knows that in the day you eat of it your eyes will be opened and you will be like God, knowing good and evil" (Genesis 3:4-5).

The choice was between believing who was lying—God or the serpent. The serpent's trap was to convince the husband and wife they were missing out on something good as a result of innocently trusting God. If they ate, their eyes would be opened. The striking statement is that the result would be that they would be "like God, knowing good and evil." God was keeping them naïve, the serpent explained. The woman bought into the serpent's enticement, convinced God was preventing them from something very beneficial. The husband and the wife wanted to have as much knowledge as God had. They didn't want any limits to their knowledge. They wanted to be omniscient. That is what led to the breakdown in communication and judgment.

In Genesis 11, the people wanted to build a city to glorify humanity: "'Come, let us build ourselves a city, and a tower whose top is in the heavens; let us make a name for ourselves, lest we be scattered abroad over the face of the whole earth.' But the Lord came down to see the city and the tower which the sons of men had built. And the Lord said, 'Indeed the people are one and they all have one language, and this is what they begin to do; now nothing that they propose to do will be withheld from them. Come, let Us go down and there confuse their language, that they may not understand one another's speech.' So the Lord scattered them abroad from there over the face of all the earth, and they ceased building the city" (Genesis 11:4-8).

The first family wanted to be omniscient, and now these descendants of Noah wanted to be almighty too and do anything they wanted to do. God understood the people's intent was to be omnipotent. But God didn't want humanity to have His attributes. He decided to stop the project. People dispersed. Multiple languages came to being, and different cultures formed. Language and cultural barriers were also created, culminating in humanity growing further and further apart from each other.

From that time on in the Bible, language is largely portrayed in a negative sense. In Deuteronomy 28:49, it is written, "The Lord will bring a nation against you from afar, from the end of the earth, as swift as the eagle flies, a nation whose language you will not understand." In Nehemiah 13:24, it is written, "And half of their children spoke the language of Ashdod, and could not speak the language of Judah, but spoke according to the language of one or the other people."

To be fair, the book of Esther takes a positive connotation of language. In Esther we see multiple languages used as a way of communication by the government of Persia (Esther 3:12; Esther 8:9). For example, the king wrote to each ethnic group in its own language: "Then he sent letters to all the king's provinces, to each province in its own script, and to every people in their own language, that each man should be master in his own house, and speak in the language of his own people" (Esther 1:22).

But from the Psalms to the book of Malachi, language is presented as a barrier to communication. "This He established in Joseph as a testimony, When He went throughout the land of Egypt, Where I heard a language I did not understand" (Psalm 81:5). Psalm 114:1 uses the phrases "when Israel went out of Egypt, The house of Jacob from a people of strange language." In Deuteronomy 28:49, it is written, "The Lord will bring a nation against you from afar, from the end of the earth, as swift as the eagle flies, a nation whose language you will not understand."

Language continues to be portrayed in a negative tone even in Isaiah. "For with stammering lips and another tongue He will speak to this people, To whom He said, 'This is the rest with which You may cause the weary to rest,' And, 'This is the refreshing'; Yet they would not hear. But the word of the Lord was to them, 'Precept upon precept, precept upon precept, Line upon line, line upon line, Here a little, there a little,' That they might go and fall backward, and be broken And snared and caught" (Isaiah 28:11-13). Other references include Isaiah 19:18; Isaiah 36:11; Jeremiah 5:15; and Ezekiel 3:5.

The "stammering lips and another tongue" mentioned in Isaiah 28 represent a barrier of communication between the speaker and the listener. God spoke to His people Israel in love and compassion in their language so there would be understanding between Him and His people. But the people would not obey and worship God with their full hearts. Therefore, God started to speak to them through a merciless Assyrian, Babylonian, Persian and Greek and Roman people in foreign languages strange to the Jews.

It was in the midst of this disobedience that Jesus paid all the debt of the world for the whole of humanity, gentile and Jew alike. Jesus came to be a bridge of reconciliation between God and humanity. Even though everyone did not repent, Jesus founded a community that was inaugurated by the arrival of the Holy Spirit on the day of Pentecost. That day, God sent His Holy Spirit to abide in the members of this new community of believers called the church of Jesus Christ. God Himself came and now lives in us.

And once more God in His wisdom wants to use a foreign language as one of the gifts of the Holy Spirit for individual and corporate worship of God. This language comes from as far away as heaven. Because of the arrival of the Holy Spirit, some are given the ability to speak in the language of angels (1 Corinthians 13:1). This language is intended mainly for use in private prayers between God and the individual praying (1 Corinthians 14:4). Even though the language is foreign, it is not a curse like foreign languages were at the time of the Assyrian invasion of Judea. Rather, it is a communication between God and the one praying.

Language in the New Testament

The day of Pentecost completely changed the trajectory of the biblical community regarding diversity, including its understanding of who is considered the people of God and differences in culture and language among believers. We see dramatic change taking place in the ministry of Peter and Paul as we read the New Testament. It all starts in Acts 2, which tells of the day the gospel was preached in fifteen languages:

> "When the day of Pentecost had fully come, they were all with one accord in one place. And suddenly there came a sound from heaven, as of a rushing mighty wind, and it filled the whole house where they were sitting. Then there appeared to them divided tongues, as of fire, and one sat upon each of them. And they were all filled with the Holy Spirit and began to speak with other tongues, as the Spirit gave them utterance. And there were dwelling in Jerusalem Jews, devout men, from every nation under heaven. And when this sound occurred, the multitude came together, and were confused, because every-

> one heard them speak in his own language. Then they were all amazed and marveled, saying to one another, 'Look, are not all these who speak Galileans? And how is it that we hear, each in our own language in which we were born? Parthians and Medes and Elamites, those dwelling in Mesopotamia, Judea and Cappadocia, Pontus and Asia, Phrygia and Pamphylia, Egypt and the parts of Libya adjoining Cyrene, visitors from Rome, both Jews and proselytes, Cretans and Arabs—we hear them speaking in our own tongues the wonderful works of God.' So they were all amazed and perplexed, saying to one another, 'Whatever could this mean?'" (Acts 2:1-12)

Each spoke different languages, yet the people heard according to their native languages and understood the message. From that day onward we see languages used positively in a variety of contexts (see Acts 14:11; Acts 21:37; Acts 21:40; Acts 22:2; Acts 26:14).

Summary of the Use of Tongues in Public Worship

I believe it is proper to summarize the "how" of the use of tongues in public worship with the words of Michael Green, a balanced Pentecostal theologian: "If the tongue speaker feels impelled to give an utterance in tongues, we can be confident that God will provide someone to interpret. If nobody is forthcoming, then the worship leader will, after due pause, go on with the service. Either someone was smothering the impulse to interpret, or the original speaker simply got it wrong, and should never have spoken in that tongue in the first place.... Ability to apologize and admit we got it wrong is one of the surest ways to grow in maturity and sensitivity to what God is really saying."[66]

Tongues spoken in private prayer edify the individual. When they are spoken in public worship and interpreted into the language of the congregation, they edify the congregation. They can also be spoken in public worship quietly or by whispering in a way that doesn't disturb others.

The congregation should be long suffering as the church learns to properly use the gifts of grace. Even though human error is inevitable, the church must encourage rather than discourage the use of the gifts of grace and take a positive approach toward giving space for the Holy Spirit as He manifests Himself in these gifts.

Chapter 9

THE GIFT OF PROPHECY

There are two types of prophecy: foretelling and forthtelling. Foretelling is predicting something in the future. We should give foretold prophecies time to take place. If a foretold prophecy is taking place right now, we should investigate immediately and find out whether it is true or false. Forthtelling, on the other hand, is telling what is taking place right now. An example is when Jesus heals a man in Luke 17:19. "And He said to him, 'Arise, go your way. Your faith has made you well.'" It seems forthtelling overlaps with the gift of revelation in different places in the Bible.

Prophecy is a message from the Holy Spirit, as it is written in 2 Peter 1:19-21: "And so we have the prophetic word confirmed, which you do well to heed as a light that shines in a dark place, until the day dawns and the morning star rises in your hearts; knowing this first, that no prophecy of Scripture is of any private interpretation, for prophecy never came by the will of man, but holy men of God spoke as they were moved by the Holy Spirit."

The prophets of the Old Testament predicted the coming of the

Christ, foretelling the sequence in which things would take place (Isaiah 7; Isaiah 9; Daniel 2:31-45). It is because of this that Paul writes that the church at Ephesus was "built on the foundation of the apostles and prophets, Jesus Christ Himself being the chief cornerstone" (Ephesians 2:20).

There is ministry of prophecy in the New Testament too. But the messages of those prophets did not become a foundation like the prophecies of the Old Testament did. The purpose of prophecy in New Testament times was to encourage, to rebuke, and to edify (1 Corinthians 14:3; 1 Corinthians 14:24). In Acts 11:27-30 we read: "And in these days prophets came from Jerusalem to Antioch. Then one of them, named Agabus, stood up and showed by the Spirit that there was going to be a great famine throughout all the world, which also happened in the days of Claudius Caesar. Then the disciples, each according to his ability, determined to send relief to the brethren dwelling in Judea. This they also did, and sent it to the elders by the hands of Barnabas and Saul." This prediction, or foretelling, was meant to mobilize gentile Christians to help their Jewish brothers and sisters in Judea.

Prophecy Must Be Discerned

Paul writes: "Do not quench the Spirit. Do not despise prophecies. Test all things; hold fast what is good. Abstain from every form of evil" (1 Thessalonians 5:19-22). We can deduce a number of principles from these verses:

1. We should stay away from anything that discourages the working of the Holy Spirit.
2. We should not look down upon the gift of prophesying.
3. All prophetic utterances must be tested. There should not be an immediate "Amen" to every prophetic utterance. Discernment should be done in the same worship service at which the prophet is speaking, as is indicated in 1 Corinthians 14:29: "Let two or three prophets speak, and let the others judge."

4. The church should accept those who pass the discernment of the word of God and those whose predictions take place as predicted.

How Do We Know Prophecy Is from God?

In charismatic circles the church faces the challenge of people wanting a place of prominence, or in some instances people who are led by demonic spirits that utter words in worship services that foretell or forthtell. How do we discern whether these utterances are from God, from a desire to be recognized, or from the influence of demonic spirits? The Bible gives us tools by which we may discern such confusing utterances.

1. Fulfillment of the prophecy

Anything foretold or forthtold in the name of God should take place. "When a prophet speaks in the name of the Lord, if the thing does not happen or come to pass, that is the thing which the Lord has not spoken; the prophet has spoken it presumptuously; you shall not be afraid of him" (Deuteronomy 18:22). God's people were told not to be afraid of what the prophet said if his prophecy did not come true. In this text we also see that people can speak in the name of God from their own presumption. Speaking in the name of the Lord presumptuously is a major offense that was punishable by death in the Old Testament. "But the prophet who presumes to speak a word in My name, which I have not commanded him to speak, or who speaks in the name of other gods, that prophet shall die" (Deuteronomy 18:20). A prediction not coming true is a major sign God did not reveal the prediction to the person who prophesied. This person should be classified as a false prophet.

2. The test of the Scriptures

"If there arises among you a prophet or a dreamer of dreams, and he gives you a sign or a wonder, and the sign or the wonder comes to pass, of which he spoke to you, saying, 'Let us go after other gods'—which you have not known—'and let us serve them,' you shall not listen to the words of that prophet or that dreamer of dreams, for the Lord your God is testing you to know whether you love the Lord your God with all your heart and with all your soul. You shall walk after the Lord your God and fear Him, and keep His commandments and obey His voice, and you shall serve Him and hold fast to Him. But that prophet or that dreamer of dreams shall be put to death, because he has spoken in order to turn you away from the Lord your God, who brought you out of the land of Egypt and redeemed you from the house of bondage, to entice you from the way in which the Lord your God commanded you to walk. So you shall put away the evil from your midst" (Deuteronomy 13:1-5).

Even if the prediction takes place, that is not enough for it to be classified as a prophecy spoken by God. This text proves that regardless of a sign or wonder coming to pass, if it takes people to idolatry, people should not listen to the words of that prophet. The people of God should reject these kinds of signs. They are a test to determine whether they really love the Lord with all their heart and soul. Every prophetic utterance should be tested against the Scriptures and God's word to be considered legitimate. The commandments of God take precedence over prediction coming true, and a prophet who entices people to break the law of God should be classified as a false prophet. In fact, in Old Testament times, a prophet who tried to mislead God's people would be put to death.

3. The life of the prophet

"Beware of false prophets, who come to you in sheep's clothing, but inwardly they are ravenous wolves. You will know them by their fruits. Do men gather grapes from thorn bushes or figs from thistles? Even so, every good tree bears good fruit, but a

> bad tree bears bad fruit. A good tree cannot bear bad fruit, nor can a bad tree bear good fruit. Every tree that does not bear good fruit is cut down and thrown into the fire. Therefore by their fruits you will know them" (Matthew 7:15-20).

These false prophets come from among the believers themselves. They are friends with people in the congregations. They speak the language of the people. They know the joys and sorrows of the people. That is why Jesus calls them "ravenous wolves" in sheep's clothing. The only thing they cannot escape is their own style of life. That is the cardinal sign that exposes them.

People who serve with the gift of prophecy should live a life worthy of their calling, as Paul advised the Ephesian Christians (Ephesians 4:1). The church should put to the test the life of the one who claims to have the gift of prophecy and discern how he or she lives both in the church and outside the church. People who claim they are prophets but do not live according to the word of God should be considered false prophets even if what they proclaim comes true and is according to the word of God. They are wolves in sheepskin whose coverings will come off sooner or later. Thieves, adulterers, fornicators, and liars have occupied the altar and misled the people of God in charismatic circles, giving the movement a bad name. The church should watch out and protect the sheep from these wolves.

4. The gift of discernment

"Let two or three prophets speak, and let the others judge" (1 Corinthians 14:29). These instructions were given to Corinthian church leaders. According to Paul, any prophetic message, whether it's encouragement, rebuke, or instruction, should not be taken as final. It must first be judged or discerned. Only after that can it be ruled legitimate. Paul's exorcism of the demon that possessed the slave girl in Philippi is a vivid example from the book of Acts that demonstrates that every message that looks truthful or encouraging is not from God. If it had not been for the gift of discernment, the slave girl's message that "these men are the servants of the Most High God, who proclaim to us the way of salvation" (Acts 16:17) could have misled the apostles, and they could have taken her as their ally. The message of the slave girl was designed to divert attention from the apostles, overshadow the gospel, and confuse listeners. But led by the Holy Spirit, Paul discerned her message was from a demon even though the content was correct. "Paul, greatly annoyed, turned and said to the spirit, 'I command you in the name of Jesus Christ to come out of her.' And he came out that very hour" (Acts 16:18). This led to persecution, but the church of Philippi was founded on such a solid foundation that it thrived.

The apostle John writes, "Beloved, do not believe every spirit, but test the spirits, whether they are of God; because many false prophets have gone out into the world" (1 John 4:1). Truthful prophets are not led by circumstances. In 1 Kings 22 a messenger of King Ahab asked the prophet Micaiah to follow the flow of the messages false prophets were speaking. "Then the messenger who had gone to call Micaiah spoke to him, saying, 'Now listen, the words of the prophets with one accord encourage the king. Please, let your word be like the word of one of them, and speak encouragement'" (1 Kings 22:13). Micaiah refused that advice and spoke the word of God, which came true.

False prophets speak from their own hearts and emotions and do not listen to advice or rebuke.

They lure others by speaking presumptuously and claiming it is prophecy, leading godly people to believe them. Some speak of what they want God to do for the person they are praying for, as if God has given them a message. Others speak from their feelings but believe what they speak really is the word of God. But these people do not have any messages from God. No matter how strongly they believe in something, what God did not speak cannot come true. The prophet Jeremiah speaks of these false prophets: "They have also healed the hurt of My people slightly, Saying, 'Peace, peace!' When there is no peace" (Jeremiah 6:14).

At other times, people who are led by different spirits speak to disturb the well-being of the congregation. Again the prophet Jeremiah claims: "And I have seen folly in the prophets of Samaria: They prophesied by Baal And caused My people Israel to err. Also I have seen a horrible thing in the prophets of Jerusalem: They commit adultery and walk in lies; They also strengthen the hands of evildoers, So that no one turns back from his wickedness. All of them are like Sodom to Me, And her inhabitants like Gomorrah" (Jeremiah 23:13-14). We cannot be supported by demons as we preach the gospel of Jesus Christ.

Chapter 10

THE GIFT OF HEALING

Right after His baptism by John the Baptist and His temptation by Satan, Jesus made His message clear, announcing, "Repent, for the kingdom of heaven is at hand" (Matthew 4:17). The first thing Jesus did as He began His ministry in Galilee was to call His first four disciples as they fished in the Sea of Galilee (Matthew 4:18-22).

Matthew summarizes what Jesus did as He traveled the country: "And Jesus went about all Galilee, teaching in their synagogues, preaching the gospel of the kingdom, and healing all kinds of sickness and all kinds of disease among the people. Then His fame went throughout all Syria; and they brought to Him all sick people who were afflicted with various diseases and torments, and those who were demon-possessed, epileptics, and paralytics; and He healed them. Great multitudes followed Him—from Galilee, and from Decapolis, Jerusalem, Judea, and beyond the Jordan" (Matthew 4:23-25). Jesus considered healing people as important as teaching and preaching the gospel. In fact, it was only after Jesus taught, preached, and healed that He sat down for His first extended discourse, as recorded in Matthew 5-7.

Mark follows the same pattern, telling of Jesus's baptism, His temptation, the calling of the disciples, and Jesus's teaching and healing (Mark 1:9-45). So does Luke (see Luke 4). The first healing in John (John 5:2) is the story of the paralytic at the pool of Bethesda. After that John writes about the healing of the blind man in chapter 9 and the raising of Lazarus from his tomb in chapter 11.

Right after the story of Pentecost in Acts 2, we read of the healing of the man lame from his mother's womb (Acts 3:2). In Acts 8 Philip healed many disabilities and exorcised demons. Peter healed sick people in Acts 9:32-43. God also healed people and disseminated His gospel through the ministry of Paul (Acts 14:9-10; Acts 16:16-18). Additional texts about Jesus's disciples healing include Acts 3:1-9; Acts 9:33-42; Acts 13:6-12; and Acts 14:8-10.

All of these miracles show us how much emphasis was given to healing in the earthly ministry of Jesus and His disciples. The coming of the kingdom of God was on display through people finding relief from their sicknesses and disabilities. There were no sick people who were not healed after Jesus or His disciples announced healing.

The Role of Obedience in Healing

Matthew 9:1-8, Mark 2:1-12, and Luke 5:17-26 all record the story of Jesus healing a paralytic. Matthew 9:6 says that Jesus said to the paralytic, "Arise, take up your bed, and go to your house." In Mark 2:9 we read that Jesus said, "Arise, take up your bed and walk." John 5:8 says that after Jesus healed a paralytic by the pool of Bethesda, He said, "Rise, take up your bed and walk." John records another occasion (John 9:7) in which Jesus healed a blind man and then commanded him, "Go, wash in the pool of Siloam."

In these texts one can hypothetically argue that if the people in the story hadn't obeyed Jesus's commands, their healing might not have actualized. Yet it would have been highly unlikely for a blind or lame man to refuse the command of Jesus, whom they pursued and pleaded with. Rather, it is likely that anyone in a desperate situation would obey any command that would lead to healing. In one case people even removed a roof so they could be in His presence.

We know that before Jesus commanded the paralytic to rise and walk, He had seen the faith of the people who had brought the paralytic to Him. I believe the paralytic man felt a release and reconciliation with God even before Jesus commanded him to arise and walk, as Jesus's first declaration to the paralytic was, "Son, your sins are forgiven you" (Mark 2:5).

The obedience of these men can be contrasted with the story of Naaman (2 Kings 5:9-14), who refused to wash in the Jordan seven times to be healed from his leprosy. We know Naaman was not a Jew and that the way leprosy and lepers were perceived among the Syrians was different from that of the Jews. We also know Naaman was the highest official in the Syrian army and that his leprosy might not have been consequential to his social, economic, religious, or political status in Syrian society. This made him not as desperate for healing as Jewish lepers would have been. So it's unfair to compare the situation of a Jewish leper to a Syrian leper. Yet later, after Naaman's servants advised him, he washed seven times in the Jordan River and was finally healed.

In all of these stories, including that of Naaman, healing had already happened from God's vantage point. But it took obedience for the healing to actualize—a simple attempt to move in the direction of the command. It is not at all difficult to obey Jesus, for of all of those who pleaded with Jesus for healing, not one person argued about how Jesus should heal them. All of them obeyed.

The Role of Faith in Healing

In the following examples of healings of the sick by the hands of Jesus, we will see how the healings happened and expose the errors of some who claim they have healing ministries. These people cause a lot of damage, blaming people who are not healed and prompting others to doubt the gift of healing. This is a disservice to the people they trick and a dishonor to the preaching of the gospel of our Lord and Savior, Jesus Christ.

When healing is announced in Jesus's ministry, it has already been established the person has faith that can receive the healing. Neither Jesus nor His disciples ever announced a healing based on a future faith.

In the Gospel of Matthew we read, "And suddenly, a woman who had a flow of blood for twelve years came from behind and touched the hem of His garment. For she said to herself, 'If only I may touch His garment, I shall be made well.' But Jesus turned around, and when He saw her He said, 'Be of good cheer, daughter; your faith has made you well.' And the woman was made well from that hour" (Matthew 9:20-22).

In this text, Jesus declared a healing that had already taken place based on the woman's past trust in Him. Take to heart—no healing declared by Jesus was unfulfilled, because Jesus had already done it in the immediate past. The healing of this woman was manifested when Jesus declared it. She knew she was healed because she physically felt in her body the flow of blood had stopped.

We also read: "When Jesus departed from there, two blind men followed Him, crying out and saying, 'Son of David, have mercy on us!' And when He had come into the house, the blind men came to Him. And Jesus said to them, 'Do you believe that I am able to do this?' They said to Him, 'Yes, Lord.' Then He touched their eyes, saying, 'According to your faith let it be to you.' And their eyes were opened" (Matthew 9:27-30). In this story too Jesus acted on a past faith and not on a future one. He asked the blind men whether they believed He could heal them, and they said, "Yes, Lord."

In Matthew 15 Jesus healed the daughter of the Syrophoenician woman. We read that He said to her: "'O woman, great is your faith! Let it be to you as you desire.' And her daughter was healed from that very hour" (Matthew 15:28). Jesus saw faith in the woman. He was not expecting her to produce faith after He declared the healing of her daughter.

Mark reports how Bartimaeus was healed outside Jericho: "Now they came to Jericho. As he went out of Jericho with His disciples and a great multitude, blind Bartimaeus, the son of Timaeus, sat by the road begging. And when he heard that it was Jesus of Nazareth, he began to cry out and say, 'Jesus, Son of David, have mercy on me!' Then many warned him to be quiet; but he cried out all the more, 'Son of David, have mercy on me!' So Jesus stood still and commanded him to be called. Then they called the blind man, saying to him, 'Be of good cheer. Rise, he is calling you.' And throwing aside his garment, he rose and came to Jesus. So Jesus answered and said to him, 'What do you want Me to do for you?' The blind man said to Him, 'Rabboni, that I may receive my sight.' Then Jesus said to him, 'Go your way; your faith has made you well.' And immediately he received his sight and followed Jesus on the road" (Mark 10:46-52).

Here, in the healing of Bartimaeus too, Jesus acted on a faith that was already present, not on a faith the subjects produced based on which Jesus would then heal them. When Jesus said to the man, "Go your way; your faith has made you well," He affirmed the man's faith in the present perfect tense. Present perfect combines the present tense and the perfect aspect used to express an event that happened in the past that has present consequences. Therefore, the faith of Bartimaeus was in the past, resulted in his immediate healing. The same pattern repeats in Luke 17 with the healing of the ten lepers and in Luke 18 with the healing of the blind man.

Everyone Jesus declared healed was truly healed. Their healing was immediate: They were healed there and then. Like the woman who was bleeding, they knew they were healed. Their healing was also evident to others. It was visible and provable. It didn't require future faith or even immediate future faith. People were not told they would be healed if they had faith; they were told their faith had healed them. Jesus had already seen they had faith or had given them faith before He healed them. He didn't pronounce healing and expect the people to respond by faith. He saw their faith and healed them.

In some cases people didn't even ask to be healed. The blind man at the side of the street in Jerusalem (John 9:1ff) didn't ask Jesus to heal him. The paralytic man Jesus healed at the pool at Bethesda (John 5:1-8) didn't plead with Jesus to heal him. Jesus healed them out of His own volition. Healing and forgiveness of sins went together. Jesus forgave people's sins before He healed them.

God heals based on present faith, not on absent faith or future faith. Paul saw the paralytic had a saving faith and healed him in Acts 14:9. Peter and John healed the paralytic at the temple in Acts 3:4 when they saw he had faith. Sometimes Jesus even healed based on the faith of the people who helped the sick person, such as when He healed the paralytic (Matthew 9:2; Mark 2:5; Luke 5:20).

None of those Jesus pronounced healed were left unhealed. Through Jesus and His apostles we see that the faith of people can capture the healing before the healing is pronounced. We read in the Gospels that Jesus helped the unbelief of the father with an epileptic son before He healed the boy. Jesus healed his son as the man wept and said, "Lord, I believe; help my unbelief!" (Mark 9:24). Therefore, faith preceded, not followed, the declaration of healing. To those who lacked faith, Jesus gave faith before healing took place, as in the healing of the epileptic son. Faith is truly a gift of God (Ephesians 2:8-10).

God doesn't heal if there is deliberate unbelief or resistance to Him. When people did not have faith, Jesus simply did not do many miracles in their town. Matthew writes about Jesus's ministry in Nazareth, "Now He did not do many mighty works there because of their unbelief" (Matthew 13:58). Mark writes: "But Jesus said to them, 'A prophet is not without honor except in his own country, among his own relatives, and in his own house.' Now He could do no mighty work there, except that He laid His hands on a few sick people and healed them. And He marveled because of their unbelief. Then He went about the villages in a circuit, teaching" (Mark 6:4-6). There is a similar text in Matthew 13:54-58.

God's chosen time to put His promises, including healing, into action should also be taken into consideration. Abraham, for example, was given a promise that did not take place for 25 years. Genesis 21:5 reports, "Now Abraham was one hundred years old when his son Isaac was born to him." But he had been given the promise of a son when he was seventy-five years old (Genesis 12:4). It took twenty-five years of patience and endurance for that promise to come true.

It was not because Abraham did not have faith in God that Sarah did not immediately conceive. It was just because it was not God's time yet. Abraham got tired of waiting for God's promise to take place (Genesis 16) and produced a son with his slave Hagar. That created a problem, but it did not stop God from fulfilling His promise at the appointed time. God makes things happen in His own time.

Declarations of Healing

In former times people didn't need to announce healings. They just prayed for sick people and God healed whomever He wanted to heal. These days people put themselves in corners when they announce healings that don't come true. To escape being considered false prophets, the announcers blame the lack of healing on the lack of faith of the sick people. But this is not substantiated anywhere in the Bible.

God's healing is immediate, complete, perfect, and verifiable. If you are not healed after someone says you are healed, the problem is not with you or with God. It is with the person who pronounces the healing. That person is lying. God didn't tell him or her you were healed. All healings announced in Jesus's name should take place. We shouldn't be fooled by people who announce a healing and then when it doesn't happen tell us it is because of a lack of faith.

It is the duty of the announcer, through his or her gifts of the Spirit, to establish if the person has faith to receive the healing. Discernment is part of the gift of prophecy and consequently of a healing announced through prophecy. If the sick person doesn't have faith, no healing should be announced.

Healing should take place immediately or within the timeframe in which it is announced. If a healing does not take place within the timeframe, it is because the announcer did not get the message from God but rather from another source. For example, if a person with the gift of healing announces a woman will have a child a year from today, the woman should give birth no later than one year from the day of the announcement. If this does not happen, the person who prophesied this is responsible for announcing something he or she did not discern.

For example, the angel of the Lord came to Abraham and announced, "I will certainly return to you according to the time of life, and behold, Sarah your wife shall have a son" (Genesis 18:10). According to this promise, "Sarah conceived and bore Abraham a son in his old age, at the set time of which God had spoken to him" (Genesis 21:2). Sarah's lack of faith and even laughter did not prevent the promise from taking place. God kept His announced promise regardless of how Abraham and Sarah responded, and His approach to keeping His promises has been consistent ever since.

Chapter 11

THE OFFICES OF MINISTRY

We will now look at the offices of ministry, which have become a subject of discussion in recent years in Ethiopian Protestant circles. This chapter is intended to help us focus on the ministries the gifts of grace enable rather than designate occupants of certain spiritual offices. In other words, we will focus on ministry rather than on the minister.

Offices of Ministry in the Old Testament

The oldest office mentioned in the Scriptures is the prophetic office. All the characters of the Old Testament, including Abraham and Enoch, were considered prophets (Genesis 20:7; Jude 14-15).
Their very lives were used as prophetic guidance by New Testament writers like Paul. Moses was a prophet God appointed; God had promised a prophet like Moses would come to lead the people (Deuteronomy 18:18). God called Elijah in a manner not explained in the Bible (1 Kings 17:1). Elisha was anointed by Elijah to become a prophet (2 Kings 19:19-21). Many prophets wrote big and small books in the Bible.

Others, like Abraham, served in the prophetic office without writing any books.

The second office in the Old Testament is the priestly office. The purpose of this office is presenting sacrifices and taking care of the tabernacle (and later the temple). We know Cain and Abel presented sacrifices. We know Noah, Abraham, and Jacob also sacrificed to the Lord. But the priestly office was not officially established until God called Aaron and his sons (Exodus 30–34). Starting from that time, the descendants of Aaron performed priestly service in the temple of the Lord.

The third office is the office of the kings. Israel did not have kings—God Himself was their king—until they demanded a king like their neighbors. When the people insisted, God commanded Samuel to anoint Saul as the first king (1 Samuel 9:1-10). When Saul disobeyed God, He commanded Samuel to anoint David (2 Samuel 16). The descendants of David held the office of the kings in the Southern Kingdom until the exile to Babylon. The Northern Kingdom was led by different kings.

There is general consensus that all three of these offices were occupied by the Messiah. Both the Old and the New Testament Scriptures testify to this fact.

"The Lord your God will raise up for you a Prophet like me from your midst, from your brethren. Him you shall hear" (Deuteronomy 18:15). Peter quotes this Scripture in Acts 3:22-23. People proclaimed "a great prophet has risen up among us" and "God has visited His people" when they saw the miracles Jesus did (Luke 7:16). Even His disciples perceived Him as "a Prophet mighty in deed and word before God and all the people" (Luke 24:19).

Hebrews 4:14-16 vividly presents Jesus in the priestly office as our High Priest: "Seeing then that we have a great High Priest who has passed through the heavens, Jesus the Son of God, let us hold fast our confession. For we do not have a High Priest who cannot sympathize with our weaknesses, but was in all points tempted as we are, yet without sin. Let us therefore come boldly to the throne of grace, that we may obtain mercy and find grace to help in time of need." We chant part of this memorable quote every Sunday in the liturgy.

All Christians are royal priesthood, and Jesus is the great High Priest. In the New Testament God sends His Son to reconcile people to Himself, and Christians are His priests, pleading with the world to be reconciled to God (2 Corinthians 5:18-21). That is what Luther called "the priesthood of all believers." In the Old Testament God smites Israel for its trespasses—for inappropriate fire for sacrifice by the children of Aaron (Leviticus 10:1-3) and for the contention over authority between Miriam and Aaron (Numbers 12:1-12). It is this royal priesthood who testifies the gospel of reconciliation to the non-Christian community and brings them to salvation and forgiveness of their sins.

Finally, the question of the Magi to King Herod as recorded in Matthew 2:2 confirms Jesus also occupied the office of the kings. "Where is He who has been born King of the Jews? For we have seen His star in the East and have come to worship Him." The Scriptures emphatically proclaim Jesus is the King of kings: "I was watching in the night visions, And behold, One like the Son of Man, Coming with the clouds of heaven! He came to the Ancient of Days, And they brought Him near before Him. Then to Him was given dominion and glory and a kingdom, That all peoples, nations, and languages should serve Him. His dominion is an everlasting dominion, Which shall not pass away, And His kingdom the one Which shall not be destroyed" (Daniel 7:13-14). The apostle Paul too calls Jesus King of kings and Lord of lords (1 Timothy 6:15).

> "I urge you in the sight of God who gives life to all things, and before Christ Jesus who witnessed the good confession before Pontius Pilate, that you keep this commandment without spot, blameless until our Lord Jesus Christ's appearing, which He will manifest in His own time, He who is the blessed and only

Potentate, the King of kings and Lord of lords, who alone has immortality, dwelling in unapproachable light, whom no man has seen or can see, to whom be honor and everlasting power. Amen" (1 Timothy 6:13-16).

Offices of Ministry in the New Testament and Their Scriptural Foundation

Christians debate how many offices there actually are—two or five. It is usual to hear teachings about fivefold offices of ministry in the New Testament based on Ephesians 4. After extended and deep study of Ephesians 4 and related texts Paul and Peter wrote about the subject, I argue there are not five but rather two offices of ministry.

At the time Ephesians was written, there were three offices of ministry because the apostles were still alive to utter testimony about Jesus's teaching and write epistles. But the foundation of their teaching was already done: Jesus Christ was the cornerstone.

The work of the apostles was done once the New Testament had been written and the apostles had died. Ephesians 2:19-22 gives us the fundamental foundation of the ministry of the New Testament: "Now, therefore, you are no longer strangers and foreigners, but fellow citizens with the saints and members of the household of God, having been built on the foundation of the apostles and prophets, Jesus Christ Himself being the chief cornerstone, in whom the whole building, being fitted together, grows into a holy temple in the Lord, in whom you also are being built together for a dwelling place of God in the Spirit."

The foundation of the prophets was the thirty-nine books of the Old Testament. The foundation Paul mentions in this passage is the verbal testimony of the apostles of Jesus Christ, for the New Testament had not been written or disseminated yet. For us today, the foundation is the written testimony of what Jesus taught and did in the presence of His apostles and what the apostles themselves left us in writing, which is included in the twenty-seven books of the New Testament. The epistles of 2 Peter and Jude, among the very last New Testament writings to be penned, exhort readers to avoid false doctrines by recalling the teachings of the apostles (2 Peter 1:12-15; 1 Peter 3:2; 1 Peter 14-16; Jude 3-4; Jude 17). Peter and Jude do not say, "Listen to the apostles living today," but instead urge believers to remember what the apostles said.

The thirty-nine books of the Old Testament were the Scriptures accepted by the Jewish synagogues. Jesus quoted the Old Testament. Paul and other apostles also quoted the Scriptures to prove their cases as they taught about the kingdom of God. The Scriptures are the foundation of universal norms for the thoughts of God: "All Scripture is given by inspiration of God, and is profitable for doctrine, for reproof, for correction, for instruction in righteousness, that the man of God may be complete, thoroughly equipped for every good work" (2 Timothy 3:16-17).

No one should quote or state doctrine or teaching contrary to the Old Testament or New Testament. Every teaching, prophecy, and vision should pass the test of the Scriptures before it is accepted by Christians. The Scriptures are the general norm against which the genuineness of all utterances, including Christian writings, sermons, and hymns, should be measured. It is the duty of pastors to protect the people in their care from false teachings and prophecies.

We cannot build a foundation on prophecies uttered after the canon was closed—that is, on prophesies that are not included in the pages of the Old and the New Testament. It was not God's intention that prophecies uttered after the closure of the canon or not included in the Bible be the foundation of any Christian teaching. Paul writes that the church of Ephesus was "built on the foundation of the apostles and prophets" (Ephesians 2:20). Teachers, preachers, and anyone serving with the gifts of utterance, including prophets, cannot start a new foundation. We cannot teach or speak anything that doesn't fit the foundation laid by the apostles of the New Testament and the prophets of the Old Testament. All teachings should be according to the Old and New Testaments. New Testament prophecies after the canon was closed should be tested against both the New Testament and the Old Testament, and even though these may be divine utterings, they cannot be used as measuring sticks or as a reference for service in Christian communities. Rather, they are for immediate edification and are uttered for immediate need in certain locality as Agabus did in Antioch. .

New Testament prophecies are for edification, exhortation, and comfort of the body of Christ, according to a number of verses in Corinthians:

> "But he who prophesies speaks edification and exhortation and comfort to men" (1 Corinthians 14:3).

> "But if all prophesy, and an unbeliever or an uninformed person comes in, he is convinced by all, he is convicted by all. And thus the secrets of his heart are revealed; and so, falling down on his face, he will worship God and report that God is truly among you. How is it then, brethren? Whenever you come together, each of you has a psalm, has a teaching, has a tongue, has a revelation, has an interpretation. Let all things be done for edification" (1 Corinthians 14:24-26).

> "For you can all prophesy one by one, that all may learn and all may be encouraged" (1 Corinthians 14:31).

The ministry of Agabus is an example of the local and limited use of New Testament prophecy: "And in these days prophets came from Jerusalem to Antioch. Then one of them, named Agabus, stood up and showed by the Spirit that there was going to be a great famine throughout all the world, which also happened in the days of Claudius Caesar. Then the disciples, each according to his ability, determined to send relief to the brethren dwelling in Judea. This they also did, and sent it to the elders by the hands of Barnabas and Saul" (Acts 11:27-30).

Agabus predicted there would be a famine throughout the world. That prophecy took place in the days of Caesar Claudius. But we don't make this prophecy the foundation of Christian teaching. Rather, it explains why Paul was raising funds throughout the churches.

Agabus also prophesied Paul would be jailed: "And as we stayed many days, a certain prophet named Agabus came down from Judea. When he had come to us, he took Paul's belt, bound his own hands and feet, and said, 'Thus says the Holy Spirit, 'So shall the Jews at Jerusalem bind the man who owns this belt, and deliver him into the hands of the Gentiles'" (Acts 21:10-11). This was so the church would know the Holy Spirit would drive Paul into a danger zone in Jerusalem.

We do not see anyone being officially installed as a prophet in the New Testament writings or practices. Yes, some people, including Agabus, were called prophets, but after the first apostles died, the church never gave qualifications for being a prophet, and no one was installed to the office of the ministry of the prophet. Now that we have discussed about prophecy, we will look at the office of the apostles.

The Office of the Apostles

The office of the apostles was an office Jesus Himself established. Here are the requirements spelled out in the New Testament to be considered a legitimate apostle:

1. Someone who had followed Jesus beginning with John's baptism through Jesus's ascension

> "Therefore, of these men who have accompanied us all the time that the Lord Jesus went in and out among us, beginning from the baptism of John to that day when He was taken up from us, one of these must become a witness with us of His resurrection" (Acts 1:21-22).

This is the first requirement the apostle Peter laid in front of the 120 followers of Jesus when they sat down to choose a man who could take the place of Judas Iscariot among the Twelve. This excluded people who became followers of Jesus after John's baptism. The man who would take the place of Judas as an apostle must have been witness to the baptism, death, resurrection, and ascension of Jesus Christ. Matthias was nominated first with this criterion and was then selected by lot according to the culture of the Jews.

2. Someone who saw Jesus after His resurrection

The apostle Paul contends with those who look down upon him as a non-apostle: "Am I not an apostle? Am I not free? Have I not seen Jesus Christ our Lord? Are you not my work in the Lord? If I am not an apostle to others, yet doubtless I am to you. For you are the seal of my apostleship in the Lord" (1 Corinthians 9:1-2).

Paul substantiates he is an authentic apostle using two pieces of evidence. He argues he saw the resurrected Lord according to the criterion stipulated by the apostle Peter (Acts 1:21-22) and that the church at Corinth was the fruit of his labor in the Lord and the seal of his apostleship. In defense of his apostleship against the false apostles, he writes, "For I consider that I am not at all inferior to the most eminent apostles. Even though I am untrained in speech, yet I am not in knowledge. But we have been thoroughly manifested among you in all things" (2 Corinthians 11:5-6).

Paul further extensively defends his apostleship in 2 Corinthians 12:11-13:

> "I have become a fool in boasting; you have compelled me. For I ought to have been commended by you; for in nothing was I behind the most eminent apostles, though I am nothing. Truly

> the signs of an apostle were accomplished among you with all perseverance, in signs and wonders and mighty deeds. For what is it in which you were inferior to other churches, except that I myself was not burdensome to you? Forgive me this wrong!"

In his message to the Galatians, Paul argues he saw the risen Lord and received a direct revelation from Him. "But I make known to you, brethren, that the gospel which was preached by me is not according to man. For I neither received it from man, nor was I taught it, but it came through the revelation of Jesus Christ" (Galatians 1:11-12).

3. Someone who was officially ordained

All apostles were required to be officially ordained and commissioned to ministry, either by Jesus Himself, by those who were themselves ordained, or by a group of dedicated ministers (as in the case of Barnabas and Saul of Tarshis). We know a multitude followed Jesus as He went from town to town and to the villages in the vicinities of those towns. Jesus knew He needed to train a small number of disciples to raise up other disciples and reach the world through the gospel of the kingdom of God. Accordingly He selected twelve disciples, which was also the number of the tribes of Israel (Matthew 19:28). Jesus installed the Twelve in front of the multitude who followed Him.

> "And He went up on the mountain and called to Him those He Himself wanted. And they came to Him. Then He appointed twelve, that they might be with Him and that He might send them out to preach, and to have power to heal sicknesses and to cast out demons: Simon, to whom He gave the name Peter; James the son of Zebedee and John the brother of James, to whom He gave the name Boanerges, that is, 'Sons of Thunder'; Andrew, Philip, Bartholomew, Matthew, Thomas, James the

son of Alphaeus, Thaddaeus, Simon the Cananite; and Judas Iscariot, who also betrayed Him. And they went into a house" (Mark 3:13-19). NU[67] adds "whom he also named apostles" before listing the names.

This official installation and designation of the apostles is recorded not only in Mark but also in Matthew 10:1-4 and Luke 6:12-16. After the death of Judas Iscariot the remaining eleven apostles understood the importance of official assignment to apostleship and installed Matthias to take the place of Judas as the twelfth apostle.

> "And in those days Peter stood up in the midst of the disciples (altogether the number of names was about a hundred and twenty), and said, 'Men and brethren, this Scripture had to be fulfilled, which the Holy Spirit spoke before by the mouth of David concerning Judas, who became a guide to those who arrested Jesus; for he was numbered with us and obtained a part in this ministry'" (Acts 1:15-17).

Peter explained further to the 120 attending the meeting in the Upper Room: "'Therefore, of these men who have accompanied us all the time that the Lord Jesus went in and out among us, beginning from the baptism of John to that day when He was taken up from us, one of these must become a witness with us of His resurrection.' And they proposed two: Joseph called Barsabas, who was surnamed Justus, and Matthias. And they prayed and said, 'You, O Lord, who know the hearts of all, show which of these two you have chosen to take part in this ministry and apostleship from which Judas by transgression fell, that he might go to his own place.' And they cast their lots, and the lot fell on Matthias. And he was numbered with the eleven apostles" (Acts 1:21-26).

We also learn the importance of public installation of apostles from the sending of Saul of Tarshis and Barnabas from Antioch for their first missionary journey.

> "Now in the church that was at Antioch there were certain prophets and teachers: Barnabas, Simeon who was called Niger, Lucius of Cyrene, Manaen who had been brought up with Herod the tetrarch, and Saul. As they ministered to the Lord and fasted, the Holy Spirit said, 'Now separate to Me Barnabas and Saul for the work to which I have called them.' Then, having fasted and prayed, and laid hands on them, they sent them away" (Acts 13:1-3).

As we study the Bible we find the word "apostle" is not restricted to the twelve apostles. For example, 1 Corinthians 15:3-8 says: "For I delivered to you first of all that which I also received: that Christ died for our sins according to the Scriptures, and that He was buried, and that He rose again the third day according to the Scriptures, and that He was seen by Cephas, then by the twelve. After that He was seen by over five hundred brethren at once, of whom the greater part remain to the present, but some have fallen asleep. After that He was seen by James, then by all the apostles. Then last of all He was seen by me also, as by one born out of due time."

In this text the risen Christ was seen by as many as five hundred disciples. But among these only Paul and James, the brother of Jesus, were called apostles. Paul calls James a pillar of the church (Galatians 2:9) and equates him in 1 Corinthians 9:5 with the apostles: "Do we have no right to take along a believing wife, as do also the other apostles, the brothers of the Lord, and Cephas?" James presided over the Council of Jerusalem (Acts 15:13), the first council of the Christian church, which decided the fundamental doctrine of justification by faith apart from works of the Law. This, along with the fact that he had seen the risen

Christ, gave James the prominence of an apostle.

Barnabas was also considered to be an apostle (Acts 4:36-37) even though the Scriptures do not write about him seeing the resurrected Lord. Romans 16:7 speaks about Andronicus and Junia: "Greet Andronicus and Junia, my countrymen and my fellow prisoners, who are of note among the apostles, who also were in Christ before me." Nothing more is known in the Scriptures about these people. But apart from James, the brother of Jesus, these men worked under the apostleship of Paul.

Although Paul speaks highly of Timothy, Titus, Sylvanus, Mark, Luke, and Epaphroditus, he never appointed any of them to be apostles. Yet, they were second generation Church leaders after the apostles to disseminate the gospel to the world. Christian organizations that picked up the commandment of Jesus to go to the nations recognized themselves as missionaries, not apostles. They called individuals and communities to Christ, expanding the boundaries of the already founded church of Jesus Christ by planting congregations on the foundation of the apostles and the prophets. Those who believed were organized into congregations, which established themselves as *ekklesia* (churches), or gatherings, in Asia Minor, Africa, and Europe. They were all members of the one universal church of Jesus Christ. The next prominent group of church leaders was church fathers not apostles. Church fathers explained the Christian faith and summarized it into understandable and easy to memorize creeds like the Apostles' and Nicene Creeds.

The Holy Spirit worked His way by giving gifts of grace to the church through individual members. The churches planted in cities in Asia Minor and Europe started to flourish. As the churches used the gifts of grace, heated debates and divisions regarding greater gifts and boasting emerged among members. Ephesians 4:11-12; 1 Corinthians 12:1-30; 1 Corinthians 14:1-40; Romans 12:1-8; Colossians 3:15-17; and 1 Peter 4:7-11 were written, mostly by Paul, to clarify, guide, and admonish church members about the right and wrong uses of the gifts of grace. Paul conveyed to the churches these were gifts of grace, not recognitions of achievement or gifts given because of the pure hearts of the recipients. He makes this clear in 1 Corinthians 4:7: "For who makes you differ from another? And what do you have that you did not receive? Now if you did indeed receive it, why do you boast as if you had not received it?"

We didn't have apostles after the first-century apostles died out. It is futile to contend there should have been apostles after the New Testament canon was closed. The calling of the apostles was to lay the foundation of the Christian faith, and they did found the church and its inviolable teaching by their verbal and written testimonies.

The apostle Paul writes, "Now, therefore, you are no longer strangers and foreigners, but fellow citizens with the saints and members of the household of God, having been built on the foundation of the apostles and prophets, Jesus Christ Himself being the chief cornerstone, in whom the whole building, being joined together, grows into a holy temple in the Lord, in whom you also are being built together for a dwelling place of God in the Spirit" (Ephesians 2:19-22). The prophets Paul mentions in verse 20 are the prophets who wrote and lived the Old Testament stories.

Paul explains the church of Ephesus had already been built on the foundation of the apostles and the prophets:

> "For we are God's fellow workers; you are God's field, you are God's building. According to the grace of God which was given to me, as a wise master builder I have laid the foundation, and another builds on it. But let each one take heed how he builds on it. For no other foundation can anyone lay than that which is laid, which is Jesus Christ. Now if anyone builds on this foundation with gold, silver, precious stones, wood, hay, straw, each one's work will become clear; for the Day will declare it, because

it will be revealed by fire; and the fire will test each one's work, of what sort it is. If anyone's work which he has built on it endures, he will receive a reward. If anyone's work is burned, he will suffer loss; but he himself will be saved, yet so as through fire" (1 Corinthians 3:9-15).

These biblical evidences confirm the apostles themselves did not have a plan to prepare successors for themselves, as there was no work left for future apostles to do. The apostles had accomplished their purpose (Ephesians 2:20).

Twofold Offices of Ministry, Not Fivefold

We know there are no longer apostles similar to the apostles who lived while the New Testament was being written and that the foundation of the church was complete at the time of the writing of Ephesians. We have also looked at 1 Corinthians 3:10-11, "For no other foundation can anyone lay than that which is laid, which is Jesus Christ. Now if anyone builds on this foundation with gold, silver, precious stones, wood, hay, straw,..." which establishes that the church was founded on the teachings of the New Testament apostles and the Old Testament prophets. Leaders may plant churches, start new ministries, or participate in missions, but the church does not call them apostles. They are pastors, missionaries, bishops, episcopos, patriarchs, or, in the case of the Roman Catholic Church, popes.

We know the Bible calls Abraham a prophet (Genesis 20:7). Enoch is also called a prophet (Jude 1:14). While people may serve as prophets in the sense of proclaiming truth, there are no longer prophets who give new revelation. The Bible is already complete. In no place in the New Testament do the Scriptures establish the office of prophets. There is only the gift of prophecy, just as there are other gifts of grace like healing, tongues, and interpretation. I have heard no one contend there is office for healing or speakers of tongues, either.

The theme of Ephesians 4:8 appears to be offices of ministry, but really it is spiritual gifts. "Therefore He says: 'When He ascended on high, He led captivity captive, And gave gifts (domata) to men.'" In 1 Corinthians 12:28-30, Paul writes: "And God has appointed these in the church: first apostles, second prophets, third teachers, after that miracles, then gifts of healings, helps, administrations, varieties of tongues. Are all apostles? Are all prophets? Are all teachers? Are all workers of miracles? Do all have gifts of healings? Do all speak with tongues? Do all interpret?"

Here, miracles, healings, and other gifts are of the same value in Paul's mind as apostleship, teaching, and the working of miracles. But he is not writing about offices, so there is no reason to disconnect five gifts (apostles, teachers, prophets, pastors, and teachers) from the rest (miracles, gifts of healings, helps, administrations, and varieties of tongues) to make them offices.

Ephesians 4:10-12 reads: "He who descended is also the One who ascended far above all the heavens, that He might fill all things. And He Himself gave some to be apostles, some prophets, some evangelists, and some pastors and teachers, for the equipping of the saints for the work of ministry, for the edifying of the body of Christ." This is just a shorter version of 1 Corinthians 12:27-31. God gave the gifts of apostleship, prophecy, evangelism, shepherding, and teaching for the equipping of the saints. The intention here is not to establish offices of ministry. Rather, it is to explain what was already going on as gifts of grace among believers were given to equip the saints. Even though the office of apostleship existed at the time, it was not Paul's intention to establish the office of the apostles that he writes about in Ephesians 4:10-12.

We know Paul sometimes wrote a long version of discourse on a subject to one church and a shorter version to the other. One of many examples is the long list of spiritual armors in Ephesians 6:10-20 and the shorter list in 1 Thessalonians 5:8. In the same way, Ephesians 4:11-12 and 1 Corinthians 12 are short and long versions of the same teachings to different churches. Paul gives a shorter list in Ephesians 4, but in 1 Corinthians 12 he gives a longer list. Even though it looks like Paul is giving a title for ministers, the section is about the gifts of grace, not about designating offices of ministry to people. Therefore, Ephesians 4:11-12 and 1 Corinthians 12:27-31 do not establish the offices of ministry. They were both written about the gifts of grace.

Church history doesn't support the designation of apostles or prophets, either. Early church leaders who followed the apostles did not call themselves apostles. They did not appoint themselves as prophets. They did not appoint other people as apostles or prophets. The church gave them the title "church fathers," for they were the first to interpret the Scriptures and explain doctrine the apostles had taught. They also established the doctrine of the Trinity summarizing the Christian faith into short and memorable creeds.

Whereas the Holy Spirit gives humility, the effort to be called apostles and prophets emanates from a selfish desire to be celebrated. God calls ministers, and they mature in their calling whether they are pastors or deacons, but there is no evidence of promotion from one office to the other. Philip, for example, was called an evangelist, but he had the gift of evangelism, or planting churches. In no place in the Bible is anyone ordained as an evangelist. In contrast, the apostle Paul was called as an apostle from the very beginning; he did not pass through a clerical hierarchy. Jesus named His twelve disciples "apostles," as immature as they were.

The popular concept of the fivefold ministry, then, appears to present a non-authentic attempt to promote church leadership, and it does so based on inaccurate interpretation of Ephesians 4:11-12. The theology behind the fivefold offices is the theology of glory. It gives hierarchy to ministers in the church. The way it has been applied in the evangelical churches of Ethiopia is a testament to this. For example, I know a pastor who was loved by many brothers and sisters who promoted himself to the position of apostle with an extended, expensive celebration. This same pastor had previously been promoted from evangelist to pastor. In one of his sermons he claimed there had been a time of evangelists, then a time of pastors, and now a time of apostles to justify why he had passed through the three offices.

If we go back to Acts 6, we see the apostles classify the work that is done in the church into just two offices:

1. The pastoral office, or the office of the shepherds, which takes over the work of prayer and the ministry of the Word based on the foundation laid by the apostles.
2. The diaconal office, or the office of the deacons, which takes care of daily necessities like service and food distribution.

First Timothy 3 and Titus 1 teach the local church is to be led by godly, qualified elders/pastors who are assisted by deacons in cooperation with the church's members. We even see this in Philippians, written in the earliest decades of the church, which is addressed "to all the saints in Christ Jesus who are in Philippi, with the bishops and deacons" (Philippians 1:1).

The Holy Spirit gives us gifts we can categorize under either the office of the shepherds or the office of the deacons. The work of evangelism is led by the pastoral office. The work of provision is done by the diaconal office. This is the biblical, New Testament model that remains applicable for today. If we serve the Lord properly with our gifts and learn from our mistakes, we will eventually exhibit maturity.

The Office of the Shepherds

The first *presbuteros*, or bishops, of the church were appointed by the apostles, as Luke notes: "And when they had preached the gospel to that city and made many disciples, they returned to Lystra, Iconium, and Antioch, strengthening the souls of the disciples, exhorting them to continue in the faith, and saying, 'We must through many tribulations enter the kingdom of God.' So when they had appointed elders in every church, and prayed with fasting, they commended them to the Lord in whom they had believed" (Acts 14:21-23).

Paul eventually gave Timothy and Titus the authority to appoint church bishops, listing the qualifications by which they should be selected from among the believers:

> "This is a faithful saying: If a man desires the position of a bishop, he desires a good work. A bishop then must be blameless, the husband of one wife, temperate, sober-minded, of good behavior, hospitable, able to teach; not given to wine, not violent, not greedy for money, but gentle, not quarrelsome, not covetous; one who rules his own house well, having his children in submission with all reverence (for if a man does not know how to rule his own house, how will he take care of the church of God?); not a novice, lest being puffed up with pride he fall into the same condemnation as the devil. Moreover he must have a good testimony among those who are outside, lest he fall into reproach and the snare of the devil (1 Timothy 3:1-7).

Similar instructions were given to Titus for the church in Crete:

> "For this reason I left you in Crete, that you should set in order the things that are lacking, and appoint elders in every city as I commanded you—if a man is blameless, the husband of one wife, having faithful children not accused of dissipation or insubordination. For a bishop must be blameless, as a steward of God, not self-willed, not quick-tempered, not given to wine, not violent, not greedy for money, but hospitable, a lover of what is good, sober-minded, just, holy, self-controlled, holding fast the faithful word as he has been taught, that he may be able, by sound doctrine, both to exhort and convict those who contradict" (Titus 1:5-9).

There were only local churches in the first century. There weren't denominations, huge central offices, synods, district offices, or parishes. Local congregations gathered in people's homes. They didn't have their own land or property. *Presbuteros* were called for life and were the present-day pastors, bishops, priest, archbishops, patriarchs, and popes. John calls them "angels of the church" in Revelation, repeating that phrase seven times for the pastors of the seven churches.

We see in Acts that pastors were officially ordained:

> "From Miletus he sent to Ephesus and called for the elders of the church. And when they had come to him, he said to them: 'You know, from the first day that I came to Asia, in what manner I always lived among you, serving the Lord with all humility, with many tears and trials which happened to me by the plotting of the Jews; how I kept back nothing that was helpful, but proclaimed it to you, and taught you publicly and from house to house, testifying to Jews, and also to Greeks, repentance toward God and faith toward our Lord Jesus Christ. And see, now I go bound in the spirit to Jerusalem, not knowing the things that will happen to me there, except that the Holy Spirit testifies in every city, saying that chains and tribulations await me. But none of these things move me; nor do I count my life dear to myself, so that I may finish my race with joy, and the ministry which I received from the Lord Jesus, to testify to the gospel of the grace of God. And indeed, now I know that you all, among whom I have gone preaching the kingdom of God, will see my face no more. Therefore I testify to you this day that I am innocent of the blood of all men. For I have not shunned to declare to you the whole counsel of God. Therefore take heed to yourselves and to all the flock, among *which the Holy Spirit has made you overseers*, [emphasis mine] to shepherd the church of God which He purchased with His own blood. For I know this, that after my departure savage wolves will come in among you, not sparing the flock. Also from among yourselves men will rise

> up, speaking perverse things, to draw away the disciples after themselves. Therefore watch, and remember that for three years I did not cease to warn everyone night and day with tears. So now, brethren, I commend you to God and to the word of His grace, which is able to build you up and give you an inheritance among all those who are sanctified.'" (Acts 20:17-32).

The office of shepherds has endured throughout history, as churches cannot be planted without a pastor taking initiative. There is no church if there is no shepherd. In the experience of the Mekane Yesus Church, most of those who planted local churches before the recognition of their calling as pastors have eventually realized their calling to the pastoral office. These ministers were trained and ordained later on. That is my experience too."

The Office of the Deacons (Acts 6:1-6; 1 Timothy 3:8; 1 Timothy 10; 1 Timothy 12; 1 Timothy 13)

Luke writes:

> "Now in those days, when the number of the disciples was multiplying, there arose a complaint against the Hebrews by the Hellenists, because their widows were neglected in the daily distribution. Then the twelve summoned the multitude of the disciples and said, 'It is not desirable that we should leave the word of God and serve tables. Therefore, brethren, seek out from among you seven men of good reputation, full of the Holy Spirit and wisdom, whom we may appoint over this business; but we will give ourselves continually to prayer and to the ministry of the word.' And the saying pleased the whole multitude. And they chose Stephen, a man full of faith and the Holy Spirit, and Philip, Prochorus, Nicanor, Timon, Parmenas, and Nicolas, a proselyte from Antioch, whom they set before

the apostles; and when they had prayed, they laid hands on them" (Acts 6:1-6).

Here, the apostles decided to separate the office of apostleship from another office they called service of tables (a reference to Acts 6:2), selecting seven men from among the believers. These had to be "men of good reputation, full of the Holy Spirit and wisdom." The congregation set the seven before the apostles, who prayed and ordained them, or laid hands on them, for this ministry.

Paul gives the designation "deacons" to these helpers. He outlines their qualifications: "Likewise deacons must be reverent, not double-tongued, not given to much wine, not greedy for money, holding the mystery of the faith with a pure conscience. But let these also first be tested; then let them serve as deacons, being found blameless. Likewise their wives must be reverent, not slanderers, temperate, faithful in all things. Let deacons be the husbands of one wife, ruling their children and their own houses well. For those who have served well as deacons obtain for themselves a good standing and great boldness in the faith which is in Christ Jesus" (1 Timothy 3:8-13).

Like pastors, deacons were officially ordained (Acts 6:1ff) and had official apostolic recognition: "Paul and Timothy, bondservants of Jesus Christ, to all the saints in Christ Jesus who are in Philippi, with the bishops and deacons" (Philippians 1:1).

Gifts Organized Under Each Office

The gifts of utterance, wisdom, and power are under the pastoral office. This is because all such gifts should be discerned through the word of God, which is the work of the pastor. He has the calling and training to discern between true and false interpretation of the Scriptures and also true and false utterances of prophecy, tongues, and healing. Therefore, prophecy, teaching, exhortation, the word of wisdom, the word of knowledge, faith, healing, miracles, discerning, tongues, interpretations, psalm, revelation, music, visions, and dreams all fall under the pastoral office (Romans 12:3-8; 1 Peter 4:7-11; 1 Corinthians 12:1-10; 1 Corinthians 14:26-33; 1 Samuel 16:15-23; 2 Kings 3:14-17; 2 Kings 14:14-15; Joel 2:28; Acts 2:17).

The gifts of ministry, generosity, and mercy (Romans 12:3-7); hospitality (1 Peter 4:7-11); and workmanship, engraving, and designing tapestry (Exodus 35:30-36:1) are included in the diaconal office, along with the administration, management, and finances of the church. In the modern church this means the upkeep of the property, utilities, and tax are the responsibility of this office.

Chapter 12

GIFTS OF GRACE AND CHRISTIAN MATURITY

Peter preaches that God gives His Spirit to those who obey Him (Acts 5:29-32). We should look closely at what it means to obey God so we will not end up congratulating ourselves as if we are given the gift of the Holy Spirit by pleasing God.

Obedience to God is not legalistic. It is not keeping the law of Moses, as Paul has already established that by the works of the law no flesh shall be justified (Galatians 2:16). Rather, those who obey God must submit to His plan of salvation as expressed in John 3:16-17: "For God so loved the world that He gave His only begotten Son, that whoever believes in Him should not perish but have everlasting life. For God did not send His Son into the world to condemn the world, but that the world through Him might be saved." We see this same theme in John 1:12—"but as many as received Him, to them He gave the right to become children of God, to those who believe in His name"—and in Acts 2:38 as Peter preaches and people believe and are baptized.

In Acts 6:7 Luke clearly writes obedience is not about ethical perfection: "Then the word of God spread, and the number of the disciples multiplied greatly in Jerusalem, and a great many of the priests were obedient to the faith."

Obedience to the faith is not obedience to the law. The priests said yes to faith in Jesus Christ as the Son of God. They believed Jesus was the Messiah Israel was waiting for.

Obedience is not about perfection according to the law, either. In Acts 3:12 we read: "So when Peter saw it, he responded to the people: 'Men of Israel, why do you marvel at this? Or why look so intently at us, as though by our own power or godliness we had made this man walk?'"

These portions of the Scriptures—and the whole context in which God gave His Spirit to His church—prove God does not give His Spirit to those who are obedient according to the law. He gives His Spirit to those who receive His Son, Jesus Christ, and are obedient to faith.

But having the gifts of grace does not guarantee maturity. The church of Corinth had every gift imaginable, yet Paul rebukes them for their immaturity: "And I, brethren, could not speak to you as to spiritual people but as to carnal, as to babes in Christ. I fed you with milk and not with solid food; for until now you were not able to receive it, and even now you are still not able; for you are still carnal. For where there are envy, strife, and divisions among you, are you not carnal and behaving like mere men?" (1 Corinthians 3:1-3). The character of immature Christians is evident in Ephesians 4:14 too, which says "we should no longer be children, tossed to and fro and carried about with every wind of doctrine, by the trickery of men, in the cunning craftiness of deceitful plotting."

Immature Christians are not set firmly on the foundation of the Scriptures. Therefore, they are tossed to and fro and are carried about with every wind of doctrine and the trickery of men. Most, though, consider themselves mature and therefore do not listen to advice from their pastors. They are infested by envy, strife, and division. Jesus tells His disciples, "I still have many things to say to you, but you cannot bear them now" (John 16:12). But the same disciples had healed the sick, preached the gospel, and raised the dead (Matthew 10:7-8). The author of Hebrews notes his readers have become "dull of hearing" (Hebrews 5:11), continuing, "For though by this time you ought to be teachers, you need someone to teach you again the first principles of the oracles of God; and you have come to need milk and not solid food. For everyone who partakes only of milk is unskilled in the word of righteousness, for he is a babe. But solid food belongs to those who are of full age, that is, those who by reason of use have their senses exercised to discern both good and evil" (Hebrews 5:12-14).

The expression of the gifts of grace, then, is not proof of Christian maturity. It is dangerous to the church when immature Christians assume leadership just because of the gifts of grace in their lives. It is evident among charismatics that God's generosity in giving gifts of grace has been misused to lead His church astray. Many have been carried away on the winds of doctrine and tricked by selfish pseudo-ministers.

Tests of Maturity

The Greek word *teleios* means "complete growth in mental and moral character." *The Hebrew-Greek Key Word Study Bible* adds that its figurative meaning in the New Testament is full-grown in mind and understanding (1 Corinthians 14:20), in knowledge of the truth (1 Corinthians 2:6; 1 Corinthians 13:10; Philippians 3:15; Hebrews 5:14), and in Christian faith and virtue (Ephesians 4:13).[68] Maturity also means doing something completely, without wavering, to the end. Mature people can take correction without offense. They benefit from counsel and even from challenges from fellow workers and opponents who wish them ill.

Peter was imperfect in his dealings in ministry. He was fearful. He was indecisive. But he is a good example for those who wish to grow in spiritual maturity. Jesus rebuked him in front of his fellow disciples after first appreciating him for his confession:

> "Simon Peter answered and said, 'You are the Christ, the Son of the living God.' Jesus answered and said to him, 'Blessed are you, Simon Bar-Jonah, for flesh and blood has not revealed this to you, but My Father who is in heaven. And I also say to you that you are Peter, and on this rock I will build My church, and the gates of Hades shall not prevail against it. And I will give you the keys of the kingdom of heaven, and whatever you bind on earth will be bound in heaven, and whatever you loose on earth will be loosed in heaven.' Then He commanded His disciples that they should tell no one that He was Jesus the Christ. From that time Jesus began to show to His disciples that He must go to Jerusalem, and suffer many things from the elders and chief priests and scribes, and be killed, and be raised the third day. Then Peter took Him aside and began to rebuke Him, saying, 'Far be it from you, Lord; this shall not happen to You!' But He turned and said to Peter, 'Get behind me, Satan! You are an offense to Me, for you are not mindful of the things of God, but the things of men'" (Matthew 16:16-23).

Yet Peter followed Jesus even after He harshly rebuked him. In another instance, Paul rebuked Peter:

> "Now when Peter had come to Antioch, I withstood him to his face, because he was to be blamed; for before certain men came from James, he would eat with the Gentiles; but when they came, he withdrew and separated himself, fearing those who were of the circumcision. And the rest of the Jews also played the hypocrite with him, so that even Barnabas was carried away with their hypocrisy. But when I saw that they were not straightforward about the truth of the gospel, I said to Peter before them all, 'If you, being a Jew, live in the manner of Gentiles and not as the Jews, why do you compel Gentiles to live as Jews?'" (Galatians 2:11-14).

But the friendship of Peter and Paul continued. In fact, in 2 Peter 3:15-16, Peter considers the writings of Paul as Scripture to be followed: "And consider that the longsuffering of our Lord is salvation—as also our beloved brother Paul, according to the wisdom given to him, has written to you, as also in all his epistles, speaking in them of these things, in which are some things hard to understand, which untaught and unstable people twist to their own destruction, as they do also the rest of the Scriptures."

Some cannot take correction at all. Those people will never mature, or if they do, it will take them a long time to come to their senses. They cannot learn from their seniors because of their own egos. Immature Christians do not have the patience to wait on God. They look for a shorter path and pray God will protect them in the shortcuts they take, which are often sinful and dishonest. Maturity, on the other hand, takes time and experience.

Paul instructs Timothy not to assign an immature Christian to leadership: "Do not lay hands on anyone hastily, nor share in other people's sins; keep yourself pure" (1 Timothy 5:22). He also says the pastor must not be "a novice, lest being puffed up with pride he fall into the same condemnation as the devil. Moreover he must have a good testimony among those who are outside, lest he fall into reproach and the snare of the devil" (1 Timothy 3:6-7).

Mature Christians know how to live with the Holy Spirit and bear fruits of the Spirit. They are capable of waiting patiently for the Lord because they trust in Him. They are sensitive and listen to the Holy Spirit in spite of what is going on around them.

Other signs of Christian maturity are having self-control against urges to move toward sexual sin, refraining from saying and doing spiritually stupid things, avoiding unnecessary verbal and physical self-defense, and having peace in the midst of chaos. In Acts 21:9-14 God wanted Paul to go to Jerusalem regardless of the persecution that awaited him there. The brothers with him wanted to avoid the pain of persecution, but Paul refused their advice and instead listened to the Holy Spirit.

The Dangers of Obvious Gifts and Miracles for the Immature Christian

Visible gifts of grace, like preaching, teaching, prophecy, tongues, interpretation, miracles, healing, words of wisdom, and words of knowledge can be dangerous if not used with humility. For the immature Christian, these gifts can lead to haughtiness and arrogance. But God is patient: "For the gifts and the calling of God are irrevocable" (Romans 11:29).

Miracles can mislead immature Christians. In the city of Samaria a sorcerer called Simon performed miracles. Simon "astonished the people of Samaria, claiming that he was someone great, to whom they all gave heed, from the least to the greatest, saying, 'This man is the great power of God.' And they heeded him because he had astonished them with his sorceries for a long time" (Acts 8:9-11).

Satan can perform miracles. The Bible says the false prophet can bring fire from the sky (Revelation 13:13). Today many people tell others their telephone numbers, names of the places from where they came, and their problems to convince them they are true prophets. But knowing the place from where someone came is not a miracle. Knowing a telephone number is not a miracle. Satan knows all this information.

But Satan cannot lead people to Christ. If you are interested in miracles, the greatest miracle is when people put their faith in Christ. The greatest miracle is when people receive Jesus Christ. That's when angels sing in heaven. What is it if you raise a dead man? He is going to die again. If you bring a person to Jesus, that person will never die but will have eternal life.

Chapter 13

THE WORKING OF THE SPIRIT IN THE LOCAL CHURCH

The apostles functioned in congregations where the Spirit was working forcefully, installing the two offices of ministry (pastors and deacons) early on to organize the gifts of the Spirit in the local congregations. There was no bureaucracy; these were local house churches. These first-century churches were very young when the apostles died.

The apostles had charismatic local congregations in mind as they passed the torch to next-generation ministers. Paul, in particular, wanted burning gifts of the Spirit in the church. We see that from the command he gives to Timothy to stir up, or rekindle, the gift of the Spirit he received through prayer and ordination (2 Timothy 1:6). The Greek word for "stir up" is *anazopurein* (αναζωπυρειν), which means "to kindle afresh, stir up the fire, fan the flame of, and gain strength"[69]

A burning gift of grace worked in Paul as he led the churches and the individuals he assigned to churches at his death. 2 Timothy is the last we hear from Paul, because he was executed in Rome a short while after he wrote this epistle.

Paul previously taught what gifts we have in the church (Romans 12; 1 Corinthians 12; 1 Corinthians 14; Ephesians 4) and how to use them in worship (1 Corinthians 14:26-30). Now he wants the gifts to burn with the Spirit. He says that without a burning Spirit it is difficult to do the fundamental work of reading, teaching, and preaching (1 Timothy 4:11-13). It should be in the midst of the burning Spirit that this work is done.

Paul reminds Timothy he received his gift (ξαρισματοσ) by words of prophecy at the time of his ordination. Both the occasion and the gift were unforgettable. It is in this context that Paul warns Timothy not to neglect (μη αμελει) his gift. When we are dull, when there is no power, we tend not to pay attention to our gifts. We slowly stop using the gifts, and they atrophy from lack of activity.

God never takes away His gifts from us because of our weaknesses (Romans 11:29), but the gifts of grace *can* be covered under ash. They can be invisible while they are present. The Holy Spirit can be quenched in our lives, because all God's activities are based on our will.

The gifts of grace work where saints are gathered together. Jesus had in His view the gathering of believers when He said: "Assuredly, I say to you, whatever you bind on earth will be bound in heaven, and whatever you loose on earth will be loosed in heaven. Again I say to you that if two of you agree on earth concerning anything that they ask, it will be done for them by My Father in heaven. For where two or three are gathered together in My name, I am there in the midst of them" (Matthew 18:18-20).

The gifts of grace also work where there is yearning expectation. Texts like Acts 1:15; Acts 2:1; Acts 4:23-31; Acts 12:12; Acts 13:1-3; and Hebrews 10:19-25 show us God actively works where His people are gathered. Hebrews 10:24 encourages us to stimulate (*paraxysmon*, or παροξυσμὸν) one another. The Greek word means "convulsion and incitement to do good things."[70] It speaks of the tremendous impact one believer can have on another believer.

The gifts of grace do not work simply because we talk about them. We should be willing to gather together and practice the gifts of grace in our churches. No gift is greater than another, but one may be more beneficial than another depending on if it can be understood by the congregation. We should pray for people to be filled by the Holy Spirit. We should pray people are able to identify their gifts and that they have the courage to use them. Gifts should make us humble, not arrogant (1 Corinthians 4:6-7). There should be respect for leadership as we practice our gifts. We should assign time for such a service in our churches. All gifts of grace are meant for public worship except those given for private service, like generosity. All are meant to work for the edification of the church.

Conclusion

All of us charismatics consider ourselves strictly biblical in our understanding of the Scriptures. Yet several groups are labeled "charismatic." While some brothers and sisters consider the label suspicious even though they accept charismatics of their particular denomination for the sake of church politics, there is a lot of suspicion among charismatics themselves. This is mainly because charismatics belong to different denominations, and therefore their understanding on important issues of Christian faith is different. Pentecostals, Baptists, Methodists, Reformed Episcopalians, and Lutherans all follow different dogmas. Charismatics, simply defined, are *Christians* of different denominations who practice gifts of grace in their respective denominations. Charismatics practice and yearn for more power and manifestation of gifts of grace in every worship service of their denominations.

Charismatic gifts of grace are gifts the Holy Spirit bestows on the church of Jesus Christ. The Holy Spirit Himself and the gifts of grace do not belong to any one denomination. The church has forgotten the gifts of grace have been working in its services all of its existence. There can't be any church service without the charismatic gifts of preaching, teaching, and singing.

Gifts like prophecy are wrongly assumed to have been replaced by preaching and teaching, and gifts like tongues, interpretation, healing, and exorcism have been shunned by the church for many centuries. These gifts eventually fade away as their use becomes rare or discontinued. Yet all the gifts of grace are intended to be used for the edification and building up of the church through the generosity of God.

On continents like Africa and Asia, gifts like healing, prophecy, tongues, interpretation, and exorcism have reemerged. Even though these gifts first reemerged in California in the 1900s, they are now more prevalent in Africa. Gifts like exorcism are frequently used as demonic spirits are encountered in communities the gospel has never reached before.

It is my earnest prayer that the Western church will embrace the good intentions of charismatic Christians from the Southern Hemisphere. We must pray that the proper use of the gifts of grace will win the day among charismatics. I am optimistic, because the gospel that has been manifested through the gifts of grace in cultures throughout the world cannot be stopped by resistance even from Western churches. The field of the gospel is the world, not the West or any church. Charismatic immigrants should proclaim with John Wesley: "I look upon all the world as my parish; thus far I mean, that, in whatever part of it I am, I judge it meet, right, and my bounden duty to declare unto all that are willing to hear, the glad tidings of salvation."[71] If we make the world our parish, revival will come to the western church from outside its four walls.

APPENDIX

Appendix 1

THE GIFTS OF GRACE AS LISTED IN THE BIBLE

1 Corinthians 12:1-11 (one Spirit, many gifts)

- Utterance of wisdom
- Utterance of knowledge
- Faith
- Gifts of healing
- Working of miracles
- Prophecy
- Discerning
- Tongues
- Interpretation of tongues

1 Corinthians 12:28

- Apostles (the gift of apostleship)
- Prophets (the gift of prophecy)
- Teachers (the gift of teaching)

- Workers of miracles (the gift of working miracles)
- Healers
- Helpers
- Administrators
- Tongue speakers
- Interpreters
- Singing (compare to 1 Chronicles 25:1-8); composing is equivalent to prophecy
- Teaching
- Revelation
- Speaking in tongues
- Interpreting the tongues

Ephesians 4:7-16

- The gift of apostleship (Apostles)
- The gift of prophecy (Prophets)
- The gift of preaching the gospel and planting local churches (Evangelists or missionaries)
- The gift of caring for people (Pastors, shepherds. *Presbuteros*)
- The gift of teaching (Teachers)

Romans 12:3-8

- Prophesying in proportion to our faith
- Serving
- Teaching
- Exhorting
- Contribution in liberality
- Giving aid with zeal
- Doing acts of mercy with cheerfulness

Gifts of grace can also be classified to the following categories:

- Gifts of utterance

- Utterance of wisdom
- Utterance of knowledge
- Prophecy
- Tongues
- Interpretation of tongues
- Teaching
- Preaching
- Exhorting

Gifts of knowledge

- Discerning and Exorcism
- Revelation

Gifts of power

- Faith
- Healing
- Working of miracles
- Exorcism (casting out demons)

Gifts of leadership and administration

- Administration
- Caring for people

Gifts of charity

- Contribution
- Giving aid

Gifts of mercy

- Doing acts of mercy
- Service

Appendix 2

LESSONS LEARNED FROM THE GIFT OF HEALING

God created a perfect world. Sickness and other vices came as a result of separation from the Lord. The first disease was sin. Therefore, sickness is part of the fallen system (Revelation 21:1-4).

1. The Lord brought disease as a discipline to disobedient nations (Deuteronomy 7:15; Exodus 15:26; Exodus 32:35). But the Lord also promised to heal His people.
2. God healed a creek in Marrah (Exodus 15:22-27).
3. God healed a spring of water in Jericho (2 Kings 2:21).
4. God promised to heal the Land of Israel (2 Chronicles 7:12-18).
5. God heals individuals from disease (Psalm 103:1-5; Psalm 147:1-3).
6. Forgiveness of sins and physical healing are mentioned together. Most of the time forgiveness of sins results in physical healings (James 5:13-18).

7. Healing was a major category of Jesus's ministry on earth (Matthew 9:32-35).

Facts about Jesus's Healings

1. Jesus healed all who asked for mercy (Mark 1:32-34; Matthew 15:30; Luke 4:40; Mark 7:37). Those who didn't have someone to bring them to Jesus or those who did not come to Jesus themselves were not healed.
2. God does not heal everyone. He refused to heal Paul (2 Corinthians 12:7-10).
3. Jesus healed people who didn't know Him (John 9:35-39; John 5:1-14; Matthew 8:28-32).
4. Jesus healed from a distance (Mark 7:24-30; Matthew 15:21-28; Matthew 8:5-13; Luke 7:1-10; John 4:46-54).
5. Jesus healed by His words (Luke 17:11-19; Mark 10:46-52).
6. Jesus healed by touching the subject (Luke 7:11-17; Mark 5:35-43; Mark 1:40-45; Mark 8:22-26; Matthew 8:14-15; Matthew 9:27-31).
7. Jesus helped the unbelief of doubters before He healed them (Mark 9:24).
8. Those who touched Jesus were healed (Matthew 9:20-22; Mark 6:53-56; Matthew 14:34-36).
9. Jesus healed a paralytic (Matthew 9:1-8).
10. Jesus restored speech (Matthew 9:32-34).
11. Jesus healed a withered hand (Matthew 12:9-13).
12. Jesus healed many (Matthew 15:29-31).
13. Jesus healed an epileptic boy (Matthew 17:14-21).
14. Jesus healed a blind man at Bethsaida by spitting on his eyes and putting His hand on him. Jesus took time with him (Mark 8:22-26).
15. Jesus healed a crippled woman. He asked nothing about her faith (Luke 13:1-17).

16. Jesus healed ten lepers (Luke 17:11-19).

Healing in the Book of Acts

The principles are the same in the book of Acts. All healings were immediate.

1. A paralyzed man was healed (Acts 3:1-10)
2. Aeneas was healed (Acts 9:32-35).
3. Dorcas was restored to life (Acts 9:36-430).
4. A slave girl was freed from demons (Acts 16:16-19).
5. People were healed through handkerchiefs (Acts 19:11-14).
6. Eutyuchus was spared from death (Acts 20:7-12).

SOURCES

Aren, Gustav. *Evangelical Pioneers in Ethiopia: The Origins of the Evangelical Church Mekane Yesus.* Stockholm: EFS Forlager, 1978.

Balehegn, Mulubrhan. "The Politics and Problems of Prosperity Party Gospel." *Ethiopia Insight.* April 4, 2021. https://www.ethiopia-insight.com/2021/04/04/the-politics-and-problems-of-prosperity-party-gospel/.

Balz, Horst and Gerhard Schneider, eds. *Exegetical Dictionary of the New Testament*, Vol. 3. Grand Rapids: William B. Eerdmans, 1993.

Birri, Debela. *Divine Plan Unfolding: The Story of Ethiopian Evangelical Church Bethel.* Minneapolis: Lutheran University Press, 2014.

Blake, John. "Predictions About the Decline of Christianity in America May Be Premature." April 9, 2023. CNN. https://www.cnn.com/2023/04/08/us/christianity-decline-easter-blake-cec/index.html.

Breen, Mike. *Covenant and Kingdom: The DNA of the Bible.* Pawleys Island, South Carolina: 3DM, 2011.

Burgess, M. Stanley, eds. Encyclopedia of Pentecostal and Charismatic Christianity. Routledge: 2006.

Burgess, M. Stanley and Gary B. McGee. *Dictionary of Pentecostal and Charismatic Movements*. Grand Rapids: Zondervan, 1988.

Collins English Dictionary—Complete & Unabridged 2012 Digital Edition. William Collins Sons & Co., 2012. https://www.dictionary.com.

Earls, Aaron. "Protestant Church Closures Outpace Openings in U.S." May 25, 2021. Lifeway Research. https://research.lifeway.com/2021/05/25/protestant-church-closures-outpace-openings-in-u-s/.

Engelland, Hans Tr. "Charismatic Gifts" in *The Encyclopedia of the Lutheran Church*, Vol. 1. Julius Bodensiek, ed. Philadelphia: Fortress, 1965.

Ethiopian Evangelical Church Mekane Yesus (EECMY) Evangelism Department. "Theological Consultation on Charismatic Movement." Addis Ababa: Mekane Yesus Seminary, 1993.

Fantahun, Arefaynie. "Preachers of Prosperity: The New Face of Ethiopian Evangelical Christianity." *Ethiopia Observer*. September 1, 2019. https://www.ethiopiaobserver.com/2019/09/01/preachers-of-prosperity-the-new-breed-of-ethiopian-evangelists/ .

Fargher, Brian. "The Charismatic Movement in Ethiopia 1960-1980." Evangelical Review of Theology, Vol. 12, No. 4. October 1988.

Ferguson, Sinclair B., David F. Wright, and J.I. Packer, eds. *New Dictionary of Theology*. Leicester, England: InterVarsity Press, 1988.

Fogi, O. Teka. "The Charismatic Movement in the EECMY: Some Doctrinal and Practical Issues, An Explorative and Evaluative Case Study, The Case of the EECMY Congregations in Nekemte." Thesis submitted to the faculty of the Ethiopian Graduate School of Theology (EGST) in partial fulfillment of the requirements of the degree of master's of theology, 2000.

Friedrich, Gerhard and Gerhard Kittel, eds. *Theological Dictionary of the New Testament*, Vol. 9. Grand Rapids: William B. Eerdmans, 1973.

Greek New Testament Dictionary. United Bible Societies, 1983.

Green, Michael. *I Believe in the Holy Spirit*. Grand Rapids: William B. Eerdmans, 2004.

Jenkins, Philip. *The Next Christendom: The Coming of Global Christianity*. New York: Oxford University Press, 2002.

Jorstad, Erling. *The Holy Spirit in Today's Church: A Handbook of the New Pentecostalism*. New York: Abingdon, 1973.

"The Lutheran Church and the Charismatic Movement: Guidelines for Congregations and Pastors." Report to the Commission on Theology and Church Relations of the Lutheran Church—Missouri Synod, 1977.

Neill, Stephen. *A History of Christian Missions*, Vol. 6. London: Penguin, 1990.

NKJV Hebrew-Greek Key Word Study Bible. Chattanooga: AMG Publishers, 2015.

Pedlar, James. "Four John Wesley quotes everyone should know." May 21, 2011 https://jamespedlar.ca/2011/05/21/four-john-wesley-quotes-everyone-should-know/.

Quebedeaux, Richard. *The New Charismatics: The Origins, Development and Significance of New-Pentecostalism*. New York: Doubleday, 1976.

Smither, Edward. *Christian Mission: A Concise Global History*. St. Bellingham, Washington: Lexham, 2019.

Strong, James. *Strong's Exhaustive Concordance of the Bible*. Peabody, Massachusetts: Hendrickson, 2009.

Tappert, Theodore G. *The Book of Concord*. Philadelphia: Fortress, 1959.

Tracy, Joseph. *The Great Awakening: A History of the Revival of Religion in the Time of Edwards and Whitefield*. Middletown, Delaware: Arcadia, 2019.

ENDNOTES

1 Hans Engelland, Tr. "Charismatic Gifts" in *The Encyclopedia of the Lutheran Church,* vol. 1, ed. Julius Bodensiek (Philadelphia: Fortress, 1965), 389.

2 "The Lutheran Church and the Charismatic Movement: Guidelines for Congregations and Pastors," Report to the Commission on Theology and Church Relations of the Lutheran Church—Missouri Synod, 1977.

3 Ibid.

4 The Ethiopian Evangelical Church Mekane Yesus (EECMY) Theology Commission, "Theological Consultation on Charismatic Movement," August 22-28, 1993.

5 Ibid, 128-129.

6 The pioneers are pastors in different synods of the EECMY in whose lives the charismatic movement started. EECMY charismatics look up to these pastors as the leaders of the movement in the Mekane Yesus Church.

7 Larry Christenson, *Dictionary of Pentecostal and Charismatic Movements,* eds. Stanley M. Burgess and Gary B. McGee (Grand Rapids: Zondervan, 1988), 111.

8 Teka Fogi, Obsa,"The Charismatic Movement in the EECMY: Some Doctrinal and Practical Issues, An Explorative and Evaluative Case Study, The Case of the EECMY Congregations in Nekemte." Thesis submitted to the faculty of the Ethiopian Graduate School of Theology (EGST). Addis Ababa, 2000.

9 Christenson, 562-565.

10 Ibid 11.

11 Ibid 114, 562-565.

12 Dale W. Brown, "Pietism" in the *New Dictionary of Theology*, eds. Sinclair B. Ferguson, David F. Wright, and J.I. Packer (Leicester, England: InterVarsity Press, 1988), 516.

13 "Pietism," *The Encyclopedia of the Lutheran Church*, 1900.

14 Ibid.

15 Ibid, 515-517.

16 Ibid, 550.

17 Joseph Tracy, *The Great Awakening: A History of the Revival of Religion in the Time of Edwards and Whitefield* (Middletown, Delaware: Arcadia, 2019).

18 Stephen Neill, *A History of Christian Missions*, vol. 6 (London: Penguin, 1990), 213-215.

19 Edward Smither, *Christian Mission: A Concise Global History* (St. Bellingham, Washington: Lexham), 157.

20 Debela Birri, *Divine Plan Unfolding: The Story of Ethiopian Evangelical Church Bethel* (Minneapolis: Lutheran University Press, 2014).

21 Gustav Aren, *Evangelical Pioneers in Ethiopia: The Origins of the Evangelical Church Mekane Yesus* (Stockholm: EFS Forlager, 1978).

22 Christenson, *Dictionary of Pentecostal and Charismatic Movements,* 1-3.

23 Vinson Synan, "Classical Pentecostalism," *Dictionary of Pentecostal and Charismatic Movements,* eds. Stanley M. Burgess and Gary B. McGee (Grand Rapids: Zondervan, 1988), 5.

24 Hans Conzelmann, *Theological Dictionary of the New Testament*, eds. Gerhard Friedrich and Gerhard Kittel, vol. 9 (William B. Eerdmans, 1973), 402.

25 Ibid, 403.

26 Ibid, 404-405.

27 Horst Balz and Gerhard Schneider, eds. *Exegetical Dictionary of the New Testament*, vol. 3 (Grand Rapids: William B. Eerdmans, 1993), 461.

28 Balz and Schneider, eds., *Exegetical Dictionary of the New Testament, 26.*

29 Burgess and McGee, *Dictionary of Pentecostal and Charismatic Movements,* 156.

30 Ibid, 155-56.

31 Brian Fargher, "The Charismatic Movement in Ethiopia 1960-1980," *Evangelical Review of Theology*, vol. 12, no. 4 (October 1988), 435.

32 Ibid, 355.

33 The soloist is not entirely new in traditional folk songs. In the Oromo culture soloists are called wallee. There were also some soloists like Solomon Araya in the Addis Ababa Mekane Yesus congregation. The Pentecostal and charismatic movements have helped people compose many new hymns and sing them solo.

34 Fargher, *Evangelical Review of Theology*, 356.

35 Burgess and McGee, *Dictionary of Pentecostal and Charismatic Movements,* 1.

36 Ibid, 4.

37 Christianson, *Dictionary of Pentecostal and Charismatic Movements, 24.*

38 Richard Quebedeaux, *The New Charismatics: The Origins, Development and Significance of New-Pentecostalism* (New York: Doubleday, 1976), 5.

39 Ibid, 4.

40 Erling Jorstad, *The Holy Spirit in Today's Church: A Handbook of the New Pentecostalism* (New York: Abingdon, 1973), 59.

41 Ibid, 63.

42 Synan, *Dictionary of Pentecostal and Charismatic Movements,* 220.

43 Russell P. Spittler,"Glossolalia," *Dictionary of Pentecostal and Charismatic Movements,* eds. Stanley M. Burgess and Gary B. McGee (Grand Rapids: Zondervan, 1988), 338-339.

44 Aaron Earls, Lifeway Research, "Protestant Church Closures Outpace Openings in U.S." https://research.lifeway.com/2021/05/25/protestant-church-closures-outpace-openings-in-u-s/ (May 25, 2021).

45 Philip Jenkins, *The Next Christendom: The Coming of Global Christianity* (New York, Oxford University Press: 2002).

46 Arefaynie Fantahun, "Preachers of Prosperity: The New Face of Ethiopian Evangelical Christianity." *Ethiopia Observer*: https://www.ethiopiaobserver.com/2019/09/01/preachers-of-prosperity-the-new-breed-of-ethiopian-evangelists/ (September 1, 2019).

47 Mulubrhan Balehegn, "The Politics and Problems of Prosperity Party Gospel." *Ethiopia Insight.* https://www.ethiopia-insight.com/2021/04/04/the-politics-and-problems-of-prosperity-party-gospel/ (April 4, 2021).

48 Jenkins, *The Next Christendom*, 79.

49 Ibid, 101.

50 Ibid.

51 Ibid, 102.

52 Ibid, 204.

53 Ibid, 205.

54 John Blake, "Predictions About the Decline of Christianity in America May Be Premature." CNN: https://www.cnn.com/2023/04/08/us/christianity-decline-easter-blake-cec/index.html (April 9, 2023).

55 Theodore G. Tappert et al., *The Book of Concord* (Philadelphia: Fortress, 1959).

56 Ibid, 19.

57 Ibid, 19-20.

58 James Strong. *Strong's Exhaustive Concordance of the Bible* (Peabody, Massachusetts: Hendrickson, 2009).

59 James Strong, Strong's Exhaustive Concordance 1886, Crusade Bible Publishers, Inc. Nashville 532160 Ibid, 4570.

61 *Greek New Testament Dictionary* (United Bible Societies, 1983).

62 Strong, *Strong's Exhaustive Concordance of the Bible*, 5321.

63 Stanley Burgess, *Encyclopedia of Pentecostal and Charismatic Christianity*.

64 Mike Breen, *Covenant and Kingdom: The DNA of the Bible* (Pawleys Island, South Carolina: 3DM, 2011).

65 "Xeno," *Collins English Dictionary—Complete & Unabridged 2012 Digital Edition* (William Collins Sons & Co, 2012), https://www.dictionary.com/browse/Xeno.

66 Michael Green, *I Believe in the Holy Spirit* (Grand Rapids: William Eerdmans, 2004), 272.

67 The modern eclectic, or "critical," text of the Greek New Testament, published in the twenty-seventh edition of the Nestle-Aland Greek New Testament (N) and in the fourth edition of the United Bible Societies' Greek New Testament (U).

68 *NKJV Hebrew-Greek Key Word Study Bible* (Chattanooga: AMG Publishers, 2015).

69 Strong's Greek Dictionary of the New Testament 329.

70 Strong's Greek Dictionary 3948.

71 James Pedlar, "Four John Wesley quotes everyone should know," https://jamespedlar.ca/2011/05/21/four-john-wesley-quotes-everyone-should-know/ (May 21, 2011).